THE
MIGHTY
WEST

THE MIGHTY WEST

THE BULLDOGS' JOURNEY FROM DAYDREAM BELIEVERS TO PREMIERSHIP HEROES

KERRIE SORAGHAN

NERO

Published by Nero,
an imprint of Schwartz Publishing Pty Ltd
Level 1, 221 Drummond Street
Carlton VIC 3053, Australia
enquiries@blackincbooks.com
www.nerobooks.com

National Library of Australia Cataloguing-in-Publication entry:
Soraghan, Kerrie, author.
The mighty west: the Bulldogs' journey from daydream believers to premiership heroes/
Kerrie Soraghan.
9781863959254 (paperback)
9781925435627 (ebook)
Western Bulldogs (Football team).
Australian football—Tournaments—Victoria.
Australian football teams—Victoria—History.

Cover design by Peter Long
Text design and typesetting by Tristan Main

*This book is dedicated to
my father, Frank Soraghan,
a rover from West Footscray.*

CONTENTS

2016: THE RIDE

2016 FINALS: 'TRY TELLING THEM THEY CAN'T'

A SCOREBOARD OMEN

It's a few minutes into the last quarter of the 2016 grand final. It's been a pulsating, frenetic match. Never more than a goal or two has separated the two teams, the Sydney Swans, and my team, the Western Bulldogs. Amid the din of 100,000 people, there's just a millisecond of calm. Time freezes as, with a shiver, I notice the score: the Swans on 54, the Dogs on 61.

Not one Bulldogs fan needs to reach for the record books to recall the significance of these numbers.

54. The year of the one and only premiership for our beloved but luckless club. Men called Ted and Charlie strode the stage, on a day so far in the past that few of us have even glimpsed it as more than blurry, nostalgic footage, with the crowd in those days even able to sit inside the boundary line. My mother was among the excited throng. It was only the third match she'd ever seen, as a 17-year-old not long arrived from Ireland. She'd queued from 3 a.m. to secure her seat and witness the magical triumph, which sent the town of Footscray

into wild celebrations of red, white and blue, and transformed her into a lifelong fan.

61. The last time that the team from Melbourne's west ever made a grand final. We were actually in front at half time; our opponents, the Hawks, had at that point never won a flag. Photos show Ted Whitten on the dais again, but this time he's energetically slapping his victorious Hawthorn counterpart on the back, congratulating his team on overrunning the Dogs in the second half to achieve their first premiership. Ted and his troops would no doubt have walked from the MCG – respected adversaries, heads held high – expecting they would be back on the big stage the next year, or at least the year after that.

That didn't happen, of course. There were decades of failure. Countless dreary seasons. Seasons when our team won just two games. Seasons when we were the butt of jokes and ridicule, in which a 10-goal loss could be celebrated as a major step forward. Tough times when our very existence was threatened, when we had to rattle tins, knock on doors and dig deep, just to keep a Footscray Football Club team out on the field.

There were seven preliminary final losses, humiliating defeats and embarrassing chokes in big games, heartache and misfortune seeping from generation to generation. Gallant champions were chaired off the field, waving to the crowd, their stories too often bywords for failure and disappointment, their dreams unfulfilled, their efforts unrewarded.

Yet here now stand our team, the Western Bulldogs, seven points ahead but with 25 minutes still to play, and those momentous numbers, 54 and 61, sending a silent message – of what, we still don't know – as the shadows begin to lengthen across the MCG.

I look around the crowd, at the thousands who, like me, had come to believe and even accept that this day would never come. We'd almost made our peace with it, the idea that such joy would never be for the likes of us.

We all have our own questions: about whether just being here is enough, whether this will be a day to always remember or another in our rollcall of bitter failure. Whether our brigade of young men and a couple of steely-eyed veterans can carry the weight of all our expectations and years of disappointment, and live up to their own dreams. What it will feel like to win, or to lose. Why 22 men running around after a funny-shaped ball with an unpredictable bounce can mean so much to us. Why football really is, as someone I can't recall once said, 'the most important unimportant thing in the world'.

2014

A TEAM
FROM THE
MIGHTY
WEST

'If the young men, the bone and sinew of our industrial borough, would only come forward and take an active interest in the game, Footscray should send a powerful team into the field.'

Williamstown Advertiser, 18 May 1878

PLACES IN MY PAST

My mother had promised me I could start coming to home games when I turned four years old. In my child's imagination, a 'home' game must mean that the footballers, much like my brother and me, played kick-to-kick in someone's backyard. And I expected this to be at the home of the only player I could name: Ted Whitten. I can still recall my amazement when the eagerly awaited day arrived and I walked for the first time into the Western Oval and saw its vast expanse of emerald-green grass.

There was a unique smell of wet duffel coats and donut vans, and something indefinably Western Oval. It may have been the plumbing. The players were tiny specks far off in the distance. They wore dressing gowns and ate oranges while they listened to Ted rev them up during the breaks. We walked up to our seats in the John Gent Stand; it was rickety even then. The Hyde Street Band marched around the oval, coins whizzing dangerously past their heads. I was entranced.

So began my journey as a fan.

In 1997, the Footscray team, by then rebranded as the Western Bulldogs, played its last game at the ground where they'd been based since 1883. Our history stretches back longer than Collingwood's. Longer even than Manchester United's.

So on a mellow autumn day in 2014, when I hear that our reserves team has resumed the Footscray name and is playing at what is now called the Whitten Oval, I know I have to be there.

As I make my way to the ground, I see many fans making the same odyssey as me, strolling in the sunshine, decked out in their gear. People are flooding the streets, flying their red, white and blue colours, spilling out from the renovated houses and swanky apartments that are making the suburb unexpectedly trendy.

I even see a bloke in Bulldogs gear swinging out of his home in Droop Street, though his gait is too jaunty and the smile on his face too broad for him to be the Coodabeen Champions' talkback caller Danny, the ultimate Bulldogs pessimist.

Approaching the oval transports me back to a day in October 1989, when I attended a defiant community rally there to save the club from extinction. A 'merger' had been announced. But nobody was fooled: our team was about to be swallowed up and absorbed into an entity to be called the Fitzroy Bulldogs.

The name was a fig leaf. The Footscray Football Club was being unceremoniously booted out of the competition. Our club had come adrift in a new landscape of television rights and the Victorian Football League's relentless thirst for expansion into new territories. The Dogs were friendless, and broke.

I'd walked towards the ground with my three little boys, all dressed in their Footscray jumpers, the youngest in his pram. I wasn't sure if I was attending a celebration or a wake. I feared our battle had already been fought and lost, that apathy about the club and indifference to its fate would prevail.

But at the Gordon and Barkly Street traffic lights, I'd watched, choked with emotion, as thousands like me converged on the ground, united by a conviction that our club could not, would not, must not die. Together we'd raised the (still) amazing sum of more than $400,000 in a single day. It was the start of a successful and still unprecedented three-week campaign to save a club. The tide of history and the relentless march of the national competition – for a few more years at least – were held at bay by the community of the west.

I haven't been inside the Whitten Oval for some time. It's been transformed. The John Gent Stand has been demolished. An impressive-looking 'Elite Learning Centre' stands at the Barkly Street end, where the locals used to assemble in howling winds and icy rain, loyal and pessimistic, staunch but resigned – often in the same game, sometimes even in the same quarter. I feel sure I'm going to be inundated, even overwhelmed, by memories of the past.

Yet there's a carnival atmosphere (but not a donut van in sight). The elusive aroma has gone. The entry is not through grimy turnstiles with surly men in blue coats, but via a spacious cafe where people are milling, waiting for their lattes. Through a wall of glass you can see the city, and the Footscray team taking on the Richmond reserves.

Parents and kids spill out on the oval, playing kick-to-kick at the half-time break. There's the familiar *thump, thump, thump* of hundreds of footies hitting the grass. It's the same turf where my father took the field in the 1950s as a young reserves player.

He was a local boy, growing up a mere four blocks from the ground. His name didn't get called out in a televised national draft; when he won the Footscray and District best-and-fairest as a 17-year-old, the club 'asked him down to train'. He was a rover; midfielders hadn't been invented yet. The *Footscray Mail* was excited about his prospects, calling him a 'natural' with a 'brilliant future'.

But Dad's timing wasn't the best. He arrived at the club in 1955, right after that solitary premiership. It was a rare strong era, a champion team that was hard to break into. While he was named on the bench a couple of times, in those days you only came on if there was an injury.

At last, family legend has it, the young bloke was told by captain-coach Charlie Sutton that he would start in the 18 that weekend. Riding his bike home from his job at the Olympic Tyre factory, Dad somehow got his wheels caught in the Maribyrnong tram tracks and fell off, breaking his ankle. The club traded him to Tongala at the end of the year. The future of the promising lad was over before it began.

Later, Dad, who was a draftsman, designed the Olympic clock, a recognisable feature of the Western Oval landscape. It's no longer there, and neither is the scoreboard, leaving an imposing emptiness on Mount Mistake Hill. I had watched the last ever senior Footscray match there, in a fittingly icy and rain-soaked finale.

I thought I'd be awash with sentiment, overwhelmed by the history and tradition of this special place, but my feelings are of curiosity, not regret. Maybe it's the balmy weather; maybe it's the unfamiliar landscape, so drastically changed that my markers have all but disappeared. Instead of being sad, I'm proud of our club's resilience, its big-hearted, welcoming place in our community.

Even though I enjoy watching our Footscray lads, who are lumbering around with comical numbers like 73 on their backs, post a big win, there's another game of footy still to be played. It's down the road at the high-tech stadium built a few years ago at Docklands. Last year Richmond thrashed us there twice, in lopsided contests. The same fate, I fear, could well be on the cards today.

A GATHERING OF THE TRUE BELIEVERS

I leave the sunny Whitten Oval behind and travel to Docklands by train, to join up with the three generations of my family assembling to watch the Dogs.

My mother, who sits on the opposite side of the ground from us, is now in her 70s. Last year the club listed all the supporters who'd attended every single home game in that season. Mum's name was among them. The youngest family member here is my niece Stephanie. She is 10, too young to have seen us play at the Whitten Oval.

Along with five other AFL club tenants (not to mention events as diverse as KISS concerts and a Papal visit), the Bulldogs now call the Docklands stadium home. I've often found the atmosphere impersonal, and any sense of home contrived and even ridiculous. When you turn up as the away team to play a fellow tenant, you see other fans in the seats you imagined were somehow yours. The Bulldogs signage hailing the 'Dougie Hawkins Wing' gets dismantled swiftly after the match. Up goes new branding, labelling what we saw as our territory the 'Matthew Lloyd' end.

It's easy to point out the many contrasts to our Footscray heartland. When a chant goes up, the crowd stamp their feet on concrete floors instead of the ramshackle John Gent timber; the roar when there's a Bulldog goal ricochets under the closed roof even on this glorious day, crashing like an ocean wave, telling me earlier than my eyes can judge that it really has gone through.

But really, the rhythm of being a supporter has barely changed. Up on the seats, down on the seats. Raucous disapproval of undeserved free kicks against our team (in other words, all of them). Nicknames and in-jokes. Silent prayerful anguish as a player lines up for a much-needed goal. Joyous release if it goes through.

Maybe the sense of place isn't actually the core of being a Bulldogs fan, as I've always thought. Our Western Oval traditions are a foundation, but they're not the only thing. Other familiar elements make up pieces of our story. Babies dressed in red, white and blue booties. Toddlers who can sing the theme song and know all the numbers by heart. The humour that's sometimes brittle and sometimes bitter. The faded mural painted by schoolchildren on the corner of St Monica's in Dynon Road, showing Footscray beating Collingwood. The fact that it somehow feels we're the only club where a player with the whimsy of Bob Murphy could belong.

Something else is far too familiar as well. With three minutes of the match to go, the Dogs have surrendered the lead they'd held all day. I can barely watch as the Tigers' full-forward, Jack Riewoldt, boots the goal that puts his side back in front and begins a celebration that is bound to lead to stirring versions of 'Yellow and Black'.

Stephanie, not yet steeled to this far from unexpected turn of events, begins to cry. I, more conditioned to such heartbreak, begin marshalling the usual excuses for the loss that now seems inevitable. We had a mere six-day break compared to the Tigers' luxurious nine. (Goddamn AFL scheduling.) Each of our three matches so far has been played in heatwave conditions. (Goddamn global warming.) We're not very good ... now I've gone too far. Next thing you know, I'll be trotting out the lamest one of all: it's only a game.

I don't believe a word of it, of course. Defeat will be bitter and galling, polluting any memories of the many surprising, wonderful moments in an exuberant Bulldogs performance. Our young guns linking up to create a goal. Jackson Macrae running like the wind. Murph putting on a vintage shimmy. Tom Liberatore (or as I call him, Libba the Second) coming fiercely to the defence of his captain, Ryan Griffen, when he was dumped on the ground. Lin Jong, who was nearly delisted after breaking his leg last year, kicking two running goals. Jordan Roughead staying on the ground for three quarters with a busted shoulder. Yet none of these will console us if we throw this match away.

The Tigers have the ball in their forward line again; they're scenting the kill. But the Dogs, out on their feet, launch a counter-attack from the backline. Our players, who must be hurting badly, somehow find the will to run, supporting each other, swarming in formation down the ground, our new recruit Stewart Crameri leading the way. Daniel Giansiracusa gets a free; it was deserved, of course. When he snaps a clever goal we hear that primal Western Oval roar.

Out of nowhere I think of a line from the movie *Chariots of Fire*: 'Then where does the power come from, to see the race to its end? It comes from within.'

When the siren goes, Macrae has just mowed down a Richmond player who is sprinting towards goal. I can't hear it amid the frenzied noise of the crowd, but I know we've won when I see a Mexican wave of my fellow fans around me jumping to their feet, arms stretched to the skies, as loud and joyous as any Western Oval crowd.

Stephanie is being crushed by her parents, aunties and uncles in a giant teary bear hug and victory dance. She's all smiles now, breaking away from us to run down to the fence and see up close the heroes in red, white and blue.

GIA'S LAST DANCE

The Richmond win was, like so many others over the years, a false dawn. The elusive second premiership is further away than ever. It's been a dreary season. Steps forward were faltering, progress quickly exposed as a mirage.

Still, there's a script for this day, the final match of another unfulfilled year. And not even I can imagine it playing out differently.

Our team will be extra motivated, determined to honour one of our heroes, Daniel Giansiracusa. This will be the 265th occasion he's run down the race wearing his number 13 jumper for the Dogs. And the last.

We are playing one of the competition's newest contrivances, Greater Western Sydney, aka GWS. They've only won eight games in the three years they've been in the competition, though with the draft concessions they've received, their future domination is just a matter of time. Still, they won't trouble us when we've so much to play for, a beloved legend to send off in style.

The Orange-Clad Acronyms (as I like to call them) are, after all, an artificial construct. A bullet point in the AFL's strategic plan. They've got stakeholders; we've got fans. History. Heart. Soul.

There'll undoubtedly be tears shed at the end, as we watch Gia carried from the ground. His best mate, Bob Murphy, will be one of those carrying him. I always find this a quaint ritual, a relic of history, big men being hoisted awkwardly on their mates' shoulders, towering above everyone like warriors. Gia will be sent off with thanks, love and respect for all he has given his club and us, his loyal supporters. Our anticipated win will be one to stash away over the summer months, when footy fades gradually from our thoughts. It will be a statement from his teammates of the respect they have for Gia, whom they now affectionately dub 'The Fossil' because of his greying hair.

Our team runs out, led by Gia and his little children, who are wearing their own number 13s. Alarmingly, though, young Otis Giansiracusa (a future tongue-twisting father-son selection) gets overcome by the Bulldogs' throng of players and stumbles; the little fella is helped up by his champion dad. Gia doesn't, as he has in his other 264 games, avoid the banner and run around it. It's just a meaningless superstition, I guess, but I shift uneasily in my seat all the same.

As expected, one team is quickly out of the blocks, moving smartly, inspired by the occasion, switched on and motivated. Unfortunately that team is not the Western Bulldogs. Perhaps a gastroenteritis bug has swept through the club over the past 24 hours. It's the only plausible explanation of why our team looks listless, disinterested, unwilling to do the hard work – we make only 18 tackles in the first half. We fumble, miss easy shots at goal, and send awful, panicked bombs into the forward line.

Crowds have moods, and develop their own atmospheric mini-climates as a game goes on. At half time there's a restless, nervous energy, a collective realisation that we could lose this. Somehow the noble words and speeches of the build-up, about Gia's band of brothers and their determination to play their hearts out, are not being matched by deeds out on the ground. I search for one succinct word that would describe how I feel. It's not unknown to me and my Bulldog fellow travellers. Embarrassment.

In the third quarter the momentum shifts at last. Belatedly, the sluggish Dogs creak into action. It's still hard going, with far too many diabolical moments where it's best to avert your eyes. Stunned at the lack of polish and class, I resolutely focus on the increasingly heroic efforts of a few who are beacons of effort and skill. Bob Murphy glides around, his face even paler than usual, his expression burning with his determination to honour his friend. Dale Morris, brave, understated, is always there, stemming the tide and mopping up the ball. And there's the kid who knows how to save his best for the right moments, the kid who's made this year bearable, the kid we've begun to call The Bont.

The pent-up emotions of this frustrating afternoon spill over into a three-quarter-time melee. While I have no idea how it started or who's to blame, the pushing and shoving gives us the pretext for some spirited booing of the Acronyms. It restores some energy to the listless, funereal atmosphere.

After the melee settles down, the mood is relief. We're two points up. Now, surely, a wave of emotion for Gia will carry us home. Sentiment and tradition are on our side, dwarfing the motivation of our manufactured, soulless rivals. After all, Gia as an individual has played more games than their entire club.

The Acronyms' piddling three-year history can't be compared to ours. For inspiration, we can dig deep, drawing on the spirits of legends like Whitten, Sutton, Grant and Johnson, as well as memories of all the times Gia has put himself on the line for his club. I can't foresee anything but a win; okay, it won't be a performance for the time vault, and it won't paper over the cracks in our list, or obscure how far away we are from finals success. But at least that limp first half will be erased from the memory bank when the siren goes and we've won the match.

It's early in the fourth quarter. We're nine points up. We should go on with it now, maybe win by four or five goals. Then everything becomes a blur. Koby Stevens fails to make the distance from 35 metres out. Jake Stringer kicks another goal, his fourth in a solid afternoon. The Bont kicks a monster from 50, showing nerves of steel; this 18-year-old kid proves he is the guy for the clutch situation. But somehow, in between these moments, the Acronyms keep coming. We've lost the lead. Somehow, we're trailing again.

Gia has the ball, 30 metres out. The crowd roars for the fairytale finish. He misses, but is involved once again moments later. He's squeezed tight against the boundary line, on an impossible angle – a place from which he has so often conjured a miraculous goal. He kicks out on the full.

I think I know it at that point. It won't be a fairytale. This match will have the usual Bulldogs knife-in-the-stomach twist. A strange vision flashes through my mind: there should be signage, with elegant calligraphy like a royal warrant, fluttering in the breeze outside the Whitten Oval: *The Western Bulldogs – Purveyors of Disappointment.*

Scores are level. The ball hurtles into our forward line. Stringer leads out for a regulation mark. We don't know it in the frantic rush, but any score he kicks will win us the game as there's only 30 seconds left. But the young gun spills the mark. The Acronyms charge down the ground and score a goal.

In ignominious moments like this, as the siren sounds, a cavalcade of missed chances and heartache, witnessed over too many years of watching the Dogs, replays itself on a continuous loop in my mind. They all coalesce, the bitter losses, the dashed hopes, the miserable thrashings, and – even worse – the 'nearly there' opportunities.

It turns out the Acronyms have a theme song. It's playing in the background as we slowly rise to our feet. The crowd, all 14,725 of us, have at least stayed to farewell Gia. This isn't, of course, the most heartbreaking loss he's played in. Nor is it the worst disappointment of his long career. Gia was there in the three years – 2008, 2009, 2010 – when we reached preliminary finals. We came closest in 2009, in a suffocating and epic struggle against the Saints. With the Dogs trailing by just a goal in the last quarter, Gia launched a tough, running shot at goal on his left foot. It hung in the air for an eternity, beneath an inky MCG sky, before fading. It was close, though. It was oh so close.

Gia and his great mate Bob Murphy, who both came to our club in 1999, share another bond. They occupy first and third places on the ladder of the 'unrewarded': the list of current AFL players who've never played in a grand final. Our former captain Matthew Boyd also features prominently in this most depressing of measures. In fact, the list of the top ten retired players who never took part in a grand final is studded with Bulldog names: Brad Johnson, Doug Hawkins, Chris Grant, Scott West, Rohan Smith.

In accordance with the script, Gia is carried from the ground by Bob; Dahlhaus is the other who bears him on his shoulders. The players are a dejected lot behind them.

Tears spill, as expected. For the unfairness of footy life, and the gallantry of the unrewarded.

LOSING CAPTAIN RYAN

There's always a lot of rumour, scuttlebutt and outlandish speculation during the footy off-season, and in particular during Trade Week. I usually tune out, nauseated by hearing the names of loyal servants of their clubs thrown around like they are just pieces on a chessboard, appalled at the way young men's lives are so carelessly disposed of, disillusioned when players who've become part of our lives casually decide they need a change of scenery, a better shot at premiership success.

So at first the news that our captain, Ryan Griffen, is walking out on our club is easily dismissed. It's bound to be a lame (and not very funny) practical joke. This one's simply too ridiculous to be true.

A few moments later this complacent disbelief is followed by the piercing realisation that – of course – of course! – it could be true. In fact, it is probably, definitely true. Because unfortunately the accident-prone Dogs have lost more than their fair share of champions over the years.

And then I realise just what it will mean. This is the thunderbolt moment. My stomach lurches as the implications are absorbed. Ryan Griffen asking for a trade isn't just any ordinary player seeking more opportunities. He is our captain, the name at the bottom of letters urging us to come along to a game, the face on the posters asking us to dig deep and become a member. When he signed a new contract with us quite recently, Ryan Griffen told us, the devoted fans, that he was 'over the moon' to have finalised his new deal. At the announcement he urged any uncommitted supporters to 'get on board' with our new membership campaign, called 'The Western Front'. We listened, fond and proud, when he professed his love for the club, telling us it had been 'fantastic' and 'unbelievable', and couldn't have done more to support him through a wretched time when his father in South Australia became ill and then died.

His stunning departure can only be viewed as a deliberate, screaming vote of no confidence in our club, and in particular in our coach, Brendan McCartney. The sinister vibes at that dreadful final-round match a few weeks earlier, when we'd looked so apathetic, unable even to get motivated enough to win for Gia, suddenly take on a different perspective.

I know, in my sinking heart, what will come next. The good ole laughing-stock Bulldogs are about to implode, and spectacularly. That it is Ryan Griffen only makes the nightmare more … well, nightmarish. This is not some bumptious bighead. I can't find the venom to label him a despicable mercenary whose opinion I can indignantly dismiss. Griff is a shy, humble country boy, affectionately described by McCartney as having a 'big brother' care and solicitude for his teammates. The kid we famously selected at number three, before Buddy Franklin, in the 2004 draft – and every Dogs fan proudly declared we were glad we did. He was the boy with the mane of hair, who thrilled us running down the wings, bouncing the ball. We would rise to our feet whenever he launched those mighty kicks at goal from outside 50 metres. 'Go Griff!'

In 2006 this carefree kid was one of the young Turks exuberantly running around on the MCG as we unexpectedly, gloriously, thrashed Collingwood in an elimination final. Footy looked like a lark to Ryan Griffen and his mates Adam Cooney and Farren Ray, a boy's own adventure. Oblivious and indifferent to our legacy of finals failure, they were just wide-eyed kids, revelling in the magic of the game.

Griffen was a great and brave player in our later, more ambitious finals tilts. In 2009 we were desolate at seeing his tears, his anguish, as he lay on the MCG grass, completely spent, when the siren sounded and we'd blown a grand final berth – again. In the years since, he's kept playing wonderful games for us. He's been an all-Australian, and won our best-and-fairest twice; he's played his 200th game, and he became our captain this year.

As I absorb the shock, I think back over the past couple of years and realise that it's been a while since we saw that carefree Ryan Griffen, with his explosive pace and dangerous shimmy. I can't, in fact, remember his last electrifying goal on the run. He's been hampered by a bad back, we've conjectured. And McCartney wants every single player to 'crack in' and become a contested ball-winner. Maybe that's been a difficult transition for a naturally attacking player like Griff.

We'd wondered, too, if he was feeling the responsibility of the captaincy. Maybe he has been battling to deal with that tedious phase in a club's fortunes known as 'rebuilding'. It must be hard to find the courage and determination to produce excellence, to play your best footy and set a standard, when so little seems to be at stake. Now, like his teammates – and like us, the fans – perhaps Ryan Griffen has had difficulty adapting to a harsher, grey-tinged reality: adjusting to the knowledge that the premiership dream is gone, and a different, but no less noble, battle lies ahead. Losing more often than not. September glories just a memory. Better times only distantly, occasionally, glimpsed on the horizon.

Now, stunningly, Ryan Griffen wants out. As the wretched news spreads like wildfire, we don't hear from him – not in person, anyway. His manager issues a bland statement, the dull business-speak words hardly a match for the gravity and emotion of this bombshell. Our club retaliates with terse, repressed fury. Our formerly beloved captain is now accused of betrayal. An awful mix of truths, mistruths and wild rumours forms a potent, disastrous brew. 'The players don't get on with the coach ... Griffen never wanted to be captain ... He's been sitting on this deal, meeting with GWS for six months behind our backs ...' The whole thing is a mess I just don't want to know about.

For unsuccessful clubs like ours, latching onto individual players' journeys and believing in their stories, their devotion to our club, has provided our measure of consolation. Without flags and silverware, we cling to the memories of Rohan Smith, Brad Johnson, Scott West, Bob Murphy, the one-club players who've shown loyalty and passion. We don't want the illusion of their single-minded commitment to our club shattered. We cherish the story of Chris Grant turning his back on a million-dollar offer from Port Adelaide because a kid sent him a letter with 20 cents taped to it. We prefer to forget that a young man from

Spotswood, Callan Ward, who played 60 games for us and was earmarked as a future captain, accepted the Acronyms' riches and now wears orange.

In the wake of Griffen's announcement, I realise we don't really know the players as we think we do. We infer their personalities, their dreams, their characters from their deeds on the field. We delude ourselves that we're close to them, marching as one, that their love for the club is infinite and immutable just because ours is. Even as footy becomes more corporatised and moves further away from its tribal origins, we like to think the hackneyed old phrase 'playing for the jumper' is still part of their motivation. We imagine that our barracking, even our presence, can lift them over the line. And that they're playing for 'us'.

We devour the clichés about players 'bleeding for the club', never thinking about what that really means: we only have the vaguest understanding of monotonous pre-season training, boring stints in rehab, concussions, shattered bones and joints that ache for days. We don't like to think a club is a mundane workplace with petty squabbles and jealousies, tedious meetings and personality clashes. We see them run out onto the 'battlefield' together, huddling closely, shoulders pressed together, in a determined band, and choose to believe what they often tell us: that they're brothers, best mates playing for each other, bound to the club by loyalty and tradition, not by contracts and money. It's a myth sold to us by clubs as they appeal to our loyalty. A myth right now in tatters.

Only a few days after Ryan Griffen's bombshell announcement, Brendan McCartney is sacked. I think of the many occasions I quelled my doubts about our direction over the last few years, how many times I've tried to trust that progress will come while watching a bafflingly slow and boring game plan, how often we clapped and applauded McCartney, the besieged coach, as he walked stony-faced down to address his troops after another lame performance.

Loyalty, stoicism, patience and unquestioning commitment are constantly asked of us as fans. Not for the first time, I feel conned.

Before too long, I feel towards Ryan Griffen the same anger and sense of betrayal as the most ferocious ranters on the internet. It's almost shocking how quickly it can happen: how ruthlessly we all shut down our feelings for this guy we said we loved, and harden our broken hearts. We don't care about Ryan Griffen right at this moment, not now that he's torn apart and stripped naked our Bulldog family. That family, however dysfunctional it's apparently been behind the scenes, will always, always, come first. Another clichéd phrase – 'The club is bigger than the individual' – suddenly has a powerful, dangerous reverberation as we reel against the hammer-blows and become the target of barbs and jokes while the footy world observes our hurt and turmoil.

When further news breaks – GWS young gun Tom Boyd has requested a trade to our club – our former captain just becomes a chess piece, one we want our club to wield to maximum effect. We want to strike back, to do something bold and audacious and un-Bulldogs like, and openly show our desperate, ferocious desire for success.

A fake standoff between GWS and ourselves quickly ends, with Boyd a Bulldog and Griffen a Giant. Our battered club has somehow staggered off the canvas and, punching and flailing blindly, landed a blow. We feel a fierce sense of triumph. We

don't care if we've 'paid too much'. We don't care about the minu-
tiae of the deal or the scorn of the media commentators at the
impertinence of the Dogs for daring to dream. We feel like we
did in 1989: that we've delivered an 'up yours' to the footy world.
We're still here, guys. Still here.

There'll be time enough to worry about whether our crazy-
brave efforts to secure Tom Boyd were right. The media are
already labelling it 'the worst deal ever'. But there will be time
enough to feel unease about whether any kid who's played only
nine games can be worth so much. Time enough to worry about
whether Tom Boyd can possibly withstand the crushing weight
of being anointed a messiah at our underachieving club. Time
enough to fear the day that rapacious clubs come hunting our
Bontempelli, Macrae and Stringer, and we are reminded again
of how easily we can be preyed upon, in this new era when contracts are worth nothing. An era we've been complicit in creating,
given our courting and landing of Tom Boyd.

There'll be time enough to be sickened by this awful October of 2014 and what it says about modern-day loyalty and ethics
and the commodification of players. Time enough to overcome
the hurt and anger when we see Ward, Griffen and their coach,
another former beloved Bulldog, Leon Cameron, posing in their
orange jumpers in a piece of GWS social media marketing,
beneath the not-so-funny caption 'Lost Dogs' Home'. Undoubtedly that seemed hilarious to some callow, smart-alecky youth
from the Acronyms' marketing team. But I wonder how Griffen
and Cameron in particular, both life members of the Bulldogs,
could ever have consented to it.

Time enough to absorb the knowledge that our Brownlow
medallist Adam Cooney has also been offloaded (or perhaps

jumped ship) to Essendon; Shaun Higgins, too, has joined the exodus. Time enough for the weary realisation that next year will most likely again be a barren one. Right now, we have no captain, no coach, and our best, most dynamic player is gone. The 'golden generation' – Cooney, Ward, Griffen, Higgins – are all elsewhere, leaving us with a handful of veterans, virtually no middle tier and some untried kids.

Already I dread our next match against GWS, when our fans will boo their former hero Griffen, who wore our number 16 guernsey 202 times. I wonder whether he'll regret his decision and the way he left our club, and I remember how we cried with him in 2009. But there'll be time enough to wonder what happened to the happy-go-lucky, long-haired kid who bounced the ball as he ran on the MCG turf. Time enough just to grieve that we have lost Ryan Griffen.

THE LIGHT THAT NEVER GOES OUT

'Football, the game, the experience, the stuff of life, it exists for us to connect with a world that's gone and the one that's coming. It enlightens, enlivens, it bores, it frustrates, it gives us tiny moments of triumph along with long tracts of failure. Truly all human life is here, for football is the power, the glory, the misery, the humanity, the laughs and the loss, forever and ever. In the lives of so many of us, football is a light that never goes out. Try and extinguish it and we'll come looking for you.'

Dave Bowler, a supporter of English soccer club West Bromwich Albion, which last won the title in 1920

Barracking for the Dogs in my family has been a way of life, never a choice, never a conscious decision and never discarded when times have been hard. The team and their prospects have been an ever-present hum in the background of our lives, our conversations, our get-togethers.

In fact, I attended my first Footscray match 'in utero'. My

mother took pride in the fact that she missed only one match for each of her four pregnancies, all of which, to her annoyance, coincided with the winter months. It didn't trouble her, standing for three hours at a time in the outer, with rain trickling down her neck, as she supported her beloved team. Whenever we pressed her for snippets about the days when we were born, her reminiscences focused on the football matches.

'You were born the day after we played Hawthorn. We lost that one by a kick. The umpiring ...!'

Even after I was granted the privilege of going with her to 'home' games, I wasn't allowed to go to those mysterious events called 'away' matches. I was intrigued and disappointed when it was explained to me that not only would I be unable to see what was going on: there could well be uncouth language and undignified behaviour.

So while my mother and aunts and uncles headed off to places with exotic-sounding names – Princes Park, Glenferrie Oval – we stayed at home with my stern Irish grandmother, who lived in the Braybrook housing commission estate. She listened to the match on the radio while cooking up a storm in anticipation of the return of the usually disappointed adults.

We'd run inside when we thought it was half time. 'What's the score, Nanna?'

'Four goals down,' she'd reply in her lilting Irish brogue. Sensing this was insufficient, she'd add: 'The bloomin' umpires are killing us!'

My grandmother never attended a game in her life.

While I was dimly aware that we didn't win all that often, as a child watching them only at our home ground, it never really mattered. There was the colour, the spectacle, the mesmerising ebbs and roars of the crowd, and Footscray teams who knew that tricky wind and stormed home to snatch victories in exciting last quarters.

I began to notice, though, that the VFL competition was dominated by the 'Big Four': Richmond, Collingwood, Carlton and Essendon. These were the successful, ruthless, well-supported clubs, forever kicking sand in our puny faces. I realised then that Footscray – small, innocuous and always languishing at the bottom of the ladder – existed at the margins of the competition. We were rarely on the television replay, had little star power, and our performances occupied few column inches.

The Big Four had bold and brash colours: yellow and black; black and white; red and black; and navy. Our red, white and blue always looked tame and inoffensive. Their supporters had intimidating chants, ferocious slogans such as: 'Eat 'em alive!' They seemed to really mean them too. On the Saturday-night replays of the blockbuster matches, their cheer squads hung over the fences, triumphantly waving giant floggers amid a hail of confetti. These clubs and their fans exuded an expectation of success and, I felt, a contempt (though perhaps it was indifference) for our suffering; ours were apologetic and introverted. Their songs thumped out, rousing and strident; ours was tinny and forlorn, even containing the line: 'We'll come out smiling, if we win or lose.' Yes, we knew our place: we were resigned to mediocrity, hiding within our shells, everyone's second-favourite team, perennially non-threatening.

As I grew older I started going to away games too. Travelling to these grounds was the first time I can remember moving out of our comfort zone in the western suburbs. I was mesmerised by the sight of prosperous leafy suburbs and wide tree-lined streets with imposing Victorian-era homes. When we travelled to Princes Park and drove through Parkville and past Melbourne University, it might as well have been Oxford or Cambridge – at least for those of us who'd grown up in the flat, featureless western landscape, dotted with dingy factories and what I always thought of as the emblem of my Deer Park home: the 'purple thistle'.

It was through football that I learnt there was such a thing as class in Melbourne. I came to understand that when I answered those quintessentially Melbourne questions 'Who do you barrack for?' and 'Where did you go to school?' with 'Footscray' and 'Christ the King, Braybrook', there was a fractionally raised eyebrow, a beat of surprise.

By the time I made it to that university, our football club's failings were fixed in my mind as a western-suburbs badge of honour. We especially despised Carlton, the establishment club. One of the founders of what we liked to call the 'Bourgeois Blues', after all, was (Sir) Redmond Barry. He'd pronounced the death sentence on Ned Kelly. And (Sir) Robert Menzies had had a specially constructed ramp installed at Princes Park, so his Bentley could glide smoothly in, giving him a vantage point from which he could watch the Bluebloods untroubled by the plebian masses.

There were no 'Sirs' recorded as barracking for the Dogs.

Years, seasons, stretched by. Tantalising glimpses of success were mixed with many more of mediocrity or downright failure. There were capitulations when, despite our club's eloquent motto, 'Cede Nullis' – Yield to None, you could be sure we could cede just about everything.

Yet, like so many other Bulldogs fans, my membership is renewed automatically each year. The club sends me an email each October, usually in the name of our captain, thanking me for being a 'Bulldog for life'. Depending on the season gone by, this description might prompt a strangled laugh that's instantly followed by a grimace. Some years it has read more like a sentence handed down by the likes of Sir Redmond Barry than an inspiring confirmation of my loyalty.

I've wondered, at times, whether it's actually the Dogs' lack of success – that noble sense of tilting at windmills – that ties me to my club. One day, not long after we'd moved away from the Whitten Oval, I'd discussed this theory with a friend, Kevin, before a match. We agreed that the romance might vanish in the unlikely event we won a premiership. Our ridiculously long wait had all the ingredients of a mythical, heroic fable, inextricably linked with our sense of ourselves as western-suburbs outsiders.

Kev and I were having this deep philosophical conversation just before one of the most feared matches in the Bulldog pantheon: the must-win game against a lowly opposition. And there was little room for such theorising at three-quarter time. The Dogs had played a stinker and, despite having entered the match red-hot favourites, were trailing St Kilda, which hadn't yet won a game that season. In the hushed interval we contemplated the repercussions of this expected failure, and eventually Kev rose to his feet and delivered an anguished soliloquy, worthy of Hamlet.

'How long have I been watching this – this crap! At least at the Western Oval, we had mud. Open the roof! Bring back the mud! This is like that Leunig cartoon. A bloke goes into a tattoo shop and asks to get "Born Loser". He ends up with "Born Looser". But he says to the tattooist, "Leave it there, it's all right." Yes, that's what barracking for this mob is like.'

Kev underestimated the Dogs, at least on this occasion. We stormed home to somehow nab the four points. It was the Saints fans, our soulmates in failure and anguish, who on this occasion were left lamenting. It's gone down in history, that match, as the one where Saints defender Max Hudghton cried. Max walked off the field with tears streaming down his cheeks, inconsolable in the face of his team's meek capitulation.

At the Whitten Oval the final siren would have been the signal not just for leaps of joy that we'd pinched the game, but also for thousands of kids to leap the fence and pour onto the ground, an indulgence strictly forbidden at our new home. There, kids jostled with their heroes, slowly making their way off the ground, towering above the sea of excited fans, who would pat their muddy backs, smell their sweat and liniment, and marvel at how big these boy-men were up close.

I'd turned to Kev to get his thoughts on the meaning of this change. But he was hugging two mates, and belting out the club song.

The next day I'd spoken on the phone to my mother. She had been there to witness our exciting last-minute triumph, of course. She'd cut short a holiday in Perth and headed straight from the airport to the match. 'That team will be the death of me,' she said as we discussed the Dogs' nail-biting win. Mum has made this prediction many times. We know she considers it will be a noble, indeed fitting, way for her to end her days.

I realised then something I'd actually always known. It doesn't matter where the Dogs play or how many fruitless years we have to endure. We will always be there, the vibrant, beating heart of the game.

2015

DREAMING
TOO LOUD

'Don't dream too loud, or I'll come and shoot you ...'

*Ned Kelly's menacing advice to
a schoolteacher at the siege of Glenrowan*

ONLY 25 ROUNDS TO GO

When 2015 – season number 61 since our one and only premiership – rolls around, our club is still reeling from the disastrously messy walkout of Ryan Griffen and the chaos and ugliness surrounding the sacking of a coach. Then, in a practice match, our best-and-fairest winner Tom Liberatore, one of the few shining lights of 2014, buckles his knee. His season is over.

And yet I still eagerly await the first bounce of the ball, feeling just as much anticipation, and the same – or probably more – nervous excitement as the smugly complacent Hawks fans whose main concern is whether a fabled 'three-peat' is on the cards.

The predictions of those disappointingly pragmatic footy experts have been unanimous. In season 2015 the depleted Dogs will languish among the stragglers in the bottom four of the ladder, they say. Many of them are tipping us to add another wooden spoon to our collection.

We, the ever-devoted fans, have managed to rustle up an appropriate degree of righteous indignation at their lack of faith.

We've looked good in our pre-season hit-outs, proof that we could just surprise the tipsters, and even ourselves. (And what about The Bont?) We pore over every word of an interview with our new captain, Bob Murphy (that phrase alone puts a spring in our steps), in which he claimed that the talent of this young group exceeds that of the 2008–10 contingent, the group that came closest to a flag in recent times.

Our new coach, Luke Beveridge, is enthusiastically embraced. Our cheer squad refreshes its signs, which used to proclaim Terry Wallace as 'Our Mastermind', and which have been progressively replaced with the names Peter Rhode, Rodney Eade and, most recently, Brendan McCartney. We barely know a thing about Luke, apart from the fact that he played 30 or so games for us in the 1990s. I vaguely recall a small blur of determination in our forward line, wearing number 19 and an impressive mullet. I initiate a straw poll. Disappointingly, nobody shares my conviction that he bears a startling resemblance to the Plantagenet king Richard III.

Beveridge announces a new approach that is intriguing for us to mull over, accustomed as we had become to McCartney's focus on relentless defensive pressure.

'I don't feel you need to win 12 goals to nine or eight goals to five,' he says. 'Just so long as you win. If we kick 20 and they kick 17, we win. That's all I want. To win.'

He also decides that Matthew Boyd, a prolific midfielder but one not known for his crisp disposal skills, will be trialled in the backline. There's a few knowing smiles from the Bulldogs faithful when we hear that one. Well, at least the new bloke isn't afraid to mix it up a bit.

It's going to be a rebuilding or refreshing or renovating year, we already know that. Hundreds of games of experience have been lost. A lot is going to be left to the P-platers that form our midfield. (But what about The Bont?) It's a fair bet that as the season drags on, there are likely to be thrashings, dark days when our team of skinny striplings gets humiliated, dismal afternoons where we sit silent and stoic, days when we don't really want to get out the 'Bulldog for life' membership ticket and take our seats with fake jauntiness and black humour.

But we make our way to Docklands for Round 1 of the 2015 season with that unaccountable frisson of hope, even though we're playing a team that, unlike ours, is strongly in the frame for this year's premiership: the West Coast Eagles.

It's immediately apparent that Luke Beveridge has brought a radically new game plan. The ball hurtles from one end of the ground to another. Our team looks revitalised, an invigorated outfit, playing footy at the tempo of an exuberant Irish reel. There are daring, fast-paced handballs – audacious attempts, near-impossible at times, to link up with others in red, white and blue. When they don't come off, the noise the crowd makes is not the deflated one of disappointment, but the thrill of seeing a circus performer very nearly carry off an unlikely and risky stunt.

And, of course, there is Marcus Bontempelli.

There's a split-second of stillness in the crowd every time the 19-year-old in the number four guernsey goes near the ball. It's an anticipation, a thrilling awe, about what might and could happen.

Sometimes we daydream about where he will eventually sit in the Bulldogs pantheon. Could he be as great as Chris Grant? Does he resemble Doug Hawkins before his knee injury, with his elegant one-handed pick-ups? Or is this what it was like to see the young Ted Whitten, a mix of power and grace, a pure footballer effortlessly able to dominate in a variety of positions?

But as I watch him that Saturday night, I realise I don't want to focus on what The Bont's future might be, or whose style he most resembles. I just want to enjoy, right here and right now, what he is doing, this exceptional, once-in-a-generation talent. I want to have more of those moments, like his extraordinary blind turn and pirouette through a cluster of hapless Eagles, where he seems to freeze time. The Bont in those instants operates in some different dimension, sensing possibilities that didn't exist before – that had no right to exist at all.

Bob is interviewed by Barry Hall after we've won the match. Barry, who played his last two seasons with us, has a classically western-suburbs face. He looks every bit as big, bad and bustling as ever, though awkwardly constrained within his respectable Fox Footy suit. Bob's pretty happy with our efforts, he tells Barry, but he mentions the need to 'keep it up for the next 25 rounds'.

There is a small smile from Bob as he makes this comment, with its cheeky implication that the Dogs plan to be there on the last day in September. It's the wry smile of a guy who has made no secret of his sense of loss and mourning as he came to terms with the knowledge that a premiership would almost certainly not be among the achievements that he experienced as a player.

But I prefer to think that Bob, the great romantic, is stirred and inspired by what he sees around him, carried away for a moment by the exuberance and enthusiasm of his 'kids'. And that somewhere within that big heart, with its boundless love for our club, Bob hasn't quite given up on his dream, and is determined to do whatever it takes to be out there when our day comes.

GHOSTS OF PRELIMINARY FINALS PAST

In 1997 our team cast off the Footscray name and took the field as the Western Bulldogs. Veteran fans joked, without mirth, that this was to shake off the stigma of a diabolical 1996 season. We had only been saved from a wooden spoon by the pitiful spectacle of the moribund Fitzroy Football Club.

It wasn't, unfortunately, the worst season I'd ever seen. That dubious honour rests with the Royce Hart–coached team that managed only two wins in 1981.

But let's not downplay the credentials of '96. It was still ghoulishly awful. We'd opened the season with an 87-point thrashing. The very next week there was further humiliation when we lost to North by 131 points. Twice that season we played in front of crowds of fewer than 9000, even at our Western Oval fortress. Before too long there was a familiar spiral into turmoil, the undignified sacking of a coach, tales of infighting, whispers of schisms and treachery.

The coach who took over mid-season was Terry Wallace. He

came from Hawthorn, where brave losses and doing your best didn't cut it. He was captured on tape delivering a ferocious speech to his new charges after they'd put on a comparatively respectable showing and lost by only a goal. He cleared the room of backslappers and well-wishers and told his team that if he heard any more congratulations on a 'good effort', he would 'spew up'.

The tough love worked. The Dogs jumped out of the blocks in '97. Playing a new brand of energised, spirited footy, they finished in the top four and then ran amok in a final at the MCG, blitzing the Swans. (It was the day of Princess Diana's funeral and, for reasons that remain obscure, our cheer squad took the opportunity to offer our club's condolences to the royal family on our banner.)

Excited fans, me and my children among them, packed out training the next week to cheer our reborn team on. All that stood between us and a grand final berth – at last, after 43 years in the wilderness – was the Adelaide Crows.

At three-quarter time of that preliminary final we were 22 points up. We'd led all day. We'd played with verve, dash and commitment. We began to chatter about grand final tickets. This, surely, was our year.

A minute into the last quarter Tony Liberatore (Libba the First) snapped at goal. Our crowd rose in elation, but the goal umpire marched to the line with the customary sense of theatre and dramatically adjudged it a point. And from there the Dogs lurched into one of the more infamous of collapses. For the first time in the entire season, we failed to kick a goal in a quarter. Waves of Adelaide players streamed down the ground in sunshine which was no longer bright but vividly garish.

As sometimes happens in the worst of losses, I was unable to barrack. Any illusion that I could arrest the slide and influence the result by the intensity of my support was gone. I was a spectator in the most literal sense, and just like the dreamer unable to will their limbs to move, I was powerless and struck dumb as the quarter unfolded. We missed opportunity after opportunity to stem the tide. Our lead vanished while our players looked on, as stunned and impotent as the fans. And when the siren went and Adelaide's song blared out, we knew the full pain of what we'd lost, the ignominy of not just the defeat, but the way we'd blown it.

There are iconic pictures of that day. They have become haunting emblems of failure. Rohan Smith pounding the turf, with tears of rage and humiliation. Chris Grant's slow walk off the MCG, against a backdrop of celebrating Crows hordes. That match left scars, terrible wounds, among our supporters. No last-quarter lead was ever considered 'safe' again. No catastrophic failure was too far-fetched to be contemplated.

I call this match 'The Preliminary Final that Must Not Be Named'.

Many thought the Dogs would fall away in 1998, broken by the defeat. But we rebounded, and again finished in the top four. The '97 prelim, we decided, was one of those watersheds that premiership teams frequently endure – the heartbreak that steels a club and drives it further towards success. We told ourselves that story, even when the cards fell so that we were due to play the Crows, again, at the same venue, with the same prize at stake. We must have learnt from our mistakes. We would claim redemption.

When the siren sounded and this time the Dogs were abject losers by 63 points, our eyes were dry. At least there weren't as many 'if onlys', and no 'Was Libba's point really a goal?' controversy. But there was further damage inflicted on our fragile psyche. The Dogs couldn't be trusted. They were destined to break our hearts. My son proposed a new bumper sticker for the following season: 'Please don't hate us.'

This was 'The Other Preliminary Final that Wasn't Really Very Good Either'.

We're haunted by those lost finals, fans and (I suspect) players alike, still struggling with the idea that our club has never been able to deliver the right mix of poise, composure and daring when we need it most. In each year, the Crows, who'd joined the competition in 1991, went on to win the premiership. We've beaten them since then, yet the pain has never really faded.

The failure of '97, in particular, hovers like an unseen malevolent presence. I've often thought of it as a 'sliding doors moment', silently poisoning our later quests for a flag. If those moments had played out differently, if Terry Wallace had had the foresight, as the Crows attacked, to implement his later innovation, the 'uber-flood', in order to protect our lead, we'd have been fortified by the knowledge that we'd bravely withstood a fierce challenge and knew how to win. If, around the Whitten Oval walls, the names Johnson, West, Smith and Grant were proudly displayed as fabled premiership players, maybe then, when the blowtorch was applied in the 2008–10 era, the next generation would have drawn from their legacy of success.

Melancholy thoughts like these always swirl around in my head when we play the Crows, no matter how different the venue, the circumstances or the occasion. On this Saturday night when we take on the 'pride of South Australia', our conquerors in those awful defeats have begun the 2015 season impressively.

After three rounds they are undefeated. The Dogs have performed well so far too, but the week before, the ever professional Hawks had laid bare our inexperience and defensive fragility. We'd lost Wallis and Morris to injury. The bubble of hope and possibility could, it seemed, be about to deflate.

And yet the Dogs unleash a blitzing first quarter. They tackle like fiends. When the ball inevitably spills free, they pounce and sweep it downfield at lightning speed. They rattle on six goals; it should actually be more.

They're fast. They're daring. The arena seems wide and spacious, full of possibilities and endless green turf for Our Boys to charge into; our forwards lurk, dangerous and threatening. One moment they're locking the ball in with insane intensity, the next moment they're galloping down the ground together, waves of players running in formation.

We're up by 35 points at half time; it's a whopping 65 points at three-quarter time. We look like a top team. Like ... premiership contenders.

Early in the match there is a spine-tingling, time-capsule moment. It conveys that message from the universe that comes only in the most perfect of wins: that this is our day; that we can't possibly lose.

Clay Smith has marked the ball. He's playing his first AFL game in almost two years. Aged just 21, he's already endured two knee reconstructions, a bout of salmonella poisoning and a serious shoulder injury. It's hard to imagine the loneliness of his rehab, the despair and heaviness of each setback, the isolation and doubt, wondering whether his awful luck will ever end. But his teammates can imagine it only too well; they take the field each week knowing they are one awkward movement away from it being their story, too. They know that joy in footy is never far away from sorrow.

There seems no doubt whatsoever that Clay will kick the goal. When he does, the fans make an incredible, roof-lifting din, an outpouring of our love and goodwill. But when virtually every teammate runs to him and he gets wrapped closely in their midst, you know this is a moment for the players, and the players alone.

Meanwhile, Jake Stringer is exploding with the complete performance that he has promised but never yet quite delivered. From his very first appearance in our colours, I'd decided that only one word – *lair* – could describe him. A lair, after all, is an Australian term denoting 'a flashy man, who likes to show off', as the dictionary tells us. Jake has an aura, something threatening and electrifying and breathtaking all at once. He's catlike on his feet, he bursts through tackles, he creates a bristling force field whenever he goes near the ball. He takes his energy from the crowd, a showman loving the spotlight. (He also misses regulation set shots and drops a chest mark; perhaps these are a little mundane for one of his exceptional talent.)

Jake's all fire; his captain is more like an airy sprite, drawing on Celtic magic. Maybe Bob Murphy has played better games; if so I don't recall them. He makes the ball sing. It bounces and sits just for him, yet really that's a trick of the mind; balancing on his twinkle toes, he's perfectly attuned to what's going on, and he's intercepting it seconds before other mere mortals realise it's arrived.

And yet my favourite moment of our captain's superlative performance is not very whimsical or Bob-like at all. A Crows player is fumbling the ball near the boundary line. Bob, who is not exactly the most brutish of men, arrives simultaneously and delivers a bump that is somehow both delicate and forceful. It's easy, I think, to be misled by Bob's unlikely footy physique, and his self-effacing humour. Bob Murphy, too, is out there to win.

As we head home, my sister and I chatter excitedly, remembering wonderful moments, trying to capture again the magic and fun that this team of kids (seven of them have not yet played 20 games) are bringing us with their exuberance, their vitality. At times I expected some of them to perform cartwheels of sheer joy and enthusiasm.

We hang on every word of the radio interviews. Lin Jong says that Beveridge doesn't want them to tag their opponents; he wants his men to play their own game, 'and how much taller does that make us all walk out onto the ground?' We hear that second-gamer Lukas Webb had been practising the words of the club song, getting ready for this moment.

We could talk about it forever. And I realise that not once today have I looked back or thought about The Preliminary Final that Must Not Be Named, or The Other Preliminary Final that Wasn't Really Very Good Either.

My sister says, suddenly: 'I just think they can do it. They're going to do it, this group. They're going to win us a flag one day.'

For a fraction of a second, I think with a pang of the men who never got there. Grant and Johnson, Smith and West, and Gia. All the other men, all the other teams I've invested my hopes in, all the times that hope has faded to black. 'Yes,' I say, 'I believe it too.'

ONE MORE SONG

One day, after a match at Geelong, when Libba the First was at his pesky, annoying best, my sister and I – a petite pair – were walking out, proudly wearing our Bulldog scarves. A Geelong wit saw us, turned to his mate and rudely chortled: 'Look, it's Libba's sisters!'

The nickname has endured. And at 2 p.m. on Saturday the 'Libba Sisters' are in position on the couch, ready to watch our Dogs take on their latest challenge, the Sydney Swans. Together we will be critiquing the match and offering a balanced, fair assessment of the opposition and the umpires.

The other Libba Sister lives in an apartment in the former Rising Sun Hotel, only a few hundred metres from the Whitten Oval. Though it's been redeveloped, it still bears the quaint original signage: 'Official suppliers of beer to the Footscray Football Club.' You can hear the crowd's rumbling roar whenever our reborn Footscray team plays at its home ground.

For decades Dogs fans would spill over the Mount Mistake footbridge between the pub and the ground, gathering on

Saturday afternoons at this traditional working-class watering hole. I imagine a rambunctious atmosphere would have been the norm, as fans crowded in to celebrate the wins or obliterate their sorrows with the assistance of Footscray Football Club–sanctioned beer.

The Libba Sisters are not yet rambunctious. We're excited, tense, hopeful, expectant, uncertain. It's Round 5, and the Dogs, expected at best to have a 'rebuilding' year, have lost only one match – admittedly a belting, at the hands of the Hawks. Now the Dogs are about to face the team the Hawks vanquished in the 2014 grand final: the Swans, masters of contested footy, on their home turf.

We're fielding the least experienced team of all 18 sides selected this round. Nine of our blokes have not yet played 20 games. On average, each member of the Bulldogs outfit has played 67 fewer games than their Sydney rivals; they're also conceding three years in age, and who knows how much brawn and big match experience.

Pitted against household names like Buddy Franklin (winner of three Coleman Medals, five times an All-Australian, and a dual premiership winner) and Adam Goodes (two Brownlows, four times All-Australian, two flags) will be the likes of Fletcher Roberts, in game number eight, and Michael Talia, in game 21.

The first five minutes aren't promising as the Swans go inside 50 six times. It's a wet afternoon in the Harbour City; goals will be precious. And Franklin and Goodes look like they might go on a rampage against the fledgling Bulldog defence. So it's a relief to get on the board with virtually our first meaningful thrust forward. And a welcome surprise when we get the next.

And then, amazingly, the Dogs score the next three and have the lead at the quarter-time break.

Libba Sister 1: 'I knew we'd come back.'

Libba Sister 2: 'We'd be in front by more if the umpires would only pay all those head-high tackles.'

The second quarter is bruising. But there are heroes emerging everywhere in red, white and blue. Liam Picken, with his deceptively innocent choirboy face, loves this sort of slog; he's playing an epic game. Stewart Crameri is everywhere, with his fellow Bendigo citizen Jake Stringer wreaking his usual bull-at-a-gate mayhem. Roberts and Talia refuse to concede against their more glamorous opponents. Luke Dahlhaus is at the bottom of every pack, somehow getting boot to ball, and springing to his feet after being dumped again and again.

It's gruelling, exhausting, intense, suffocating. We're just about out on our feet at half time, completely spent from the brutal contest. Drained of energy, having given our all, we welcome the chance to regroup. There's no doubt about it: the Libba Sisters have earned their cup of tea and the sustenance of a chocolate snack.

Libba Sister 1: 'Did you notice Buddy's got a bit of a pot tummy happening?'

Libba Sister 2: 'I thought so too. Okay, so do you want a Crunchie or a Cherry Ripe?'

The Swans throw everything at the impertinent upstarts in the third quarter. We're starting to look tired, but we withstand the enormous pressure. Our players don't seem to get bowled over in tackles like they used to; even the youngest of our team is able to keep his feet and squirt a handball away.

Jordan Roughead has been switched into the ruck. With his

pale skin, old-fashioned haircut and moustache, you could imagine him wearing a slouch hat, as a resolute Anzac – a picture in a dusty frame on a mantelpiece. Both shoulders heavily bandaged from the reconstructions he has endured in his short career, he's playing a lone role against the Sydney tall timber in the waterlogged conditions, but never once does he flinch. It's an injustice, agree the indignant Libbas, when a dubious 50-metre penalty against him allows the Swans to creep within a goal in the last three minutes of the quarter.

Just as we're looking shaky, The Bont, who's demonstrated his skills are just as brilliant in the wet, shows his unerring ability to enter the game when we most need it. His octopus arms stretch out to intercept an errant Sydney kick-out. The cameras catch a close-up of his face, calm and unflustered, as he goes back to take a shot at goal. He is playing his 20th game. The Bont is not daunted by the big moment and steers it through.

The Libbas aren't sure what to think at three-quarter time. We are emotional, brimming with pride at this terrific performance, sure. But we're preparing ourselves for the prospect of being overrun. We will still be satisfied even if we end up with a brave, encouraging loss.

The Dogs are having none of the Libbas' wishy-washy notions. What follows is a last quarter for the ages. Not one player hesitates to put himself on the line, whether it's teenager and three-game veteran Lukas Webb standing in the hole as probably the best (if pot-bellied) player in the competition thunders out on a lead, or the swarm of Bulldog players who gut-run time and again, their legs burning as they get to the next contest, and the one after that.

We can't sit still on the couch anymore. Not even during the most raucous of six o'clock swills would the walls of the Rising Sun have heard such a commotion.

Despite the courage and desperation of our team, the Swans have hit the front. It epitomises this day, and the quality of our opponents, that the goal that puts them in the lead comes after a passage of play featuring multiple inspirational acts by the Dogs, and a smother from Murphy that would be match-winning in almost any other contest.

It's too frenetic to pause to ask whether the Dogs can come back. Or who among the exhausted ranks will step up to make it happen. Jason Dunstall, commentating the game, says: 'What the Dogs need now is just one special act.' For once it's not a cliché. Almost as though they've heard Dunstall's words, the Dogs will themselves forward yet again. They don't want to lose. They most definitely do not want to lose.

Luke Dahlhaus, working in space the size of a telephone box, kicks the ball towards our goal. Flying at it, with a Swan hot on his heels, is our athletic defender Easton Wood. Like Superman he leaps in the air to meet the awkwardly positioned, bouncing, spinning, greasy ball. Like Superman he gets a toe to it. It's a miraculous, brilliant goal, and the Dogs have the lead once more.

The jubilant celebrations of the Libbas are short-lived as we realise that an excruciating five minutes remains on the clock. Minutes in which a mistake could be made. Minutes in which another Special Act, this time from our more experienced and match-hardened opposition, could break our hearts.

It's a frenetic, breathless whirl of smothers, fingertips to the ball, relentless tackles. There's Bob Murphy, somehow finding something in his aching 32-year-old legs, running on pure adrenaline away from his opponent to clear it out of the danger zone. There's Jake Stringer, wrapping Buddy, who's doing his trademark fend-off, in a huge tackle, making himself a battering ram and an impassable object. There's Dahlhaus, poleaxed in a mighty, sickening clash, but seconds later back on his feet.

There's twenty seconds to go. We must surely have it won. But to our horror the Swans propel it forward once more. Twenty seconds is a long time. It's enough for a long kick down the middle. It skids into the Swans' almost vacant forward line.

'It's a footrace!' shout the commentators, as excited and involved as the rest of us.

Loping across the slippery turf into the dangerous centre-half forward zone, Easton Wood effortlessly scoops up the ball with one hand, as though it's a leisurely training drill on a calm summer's day. He keeps his balance as he's tackled and handballs to a teammate who has run hard, so very hard, in support. It's Jason Johannisen, who also holds strong in a tackle and gets the ball to Matthew Boyd. And the siren goes.

The Libbas are jumping around. All across Melbourne, our fellow Dogs fans are doing the same, yelling, screaming and crying, with joy, pride and elation – and all because Easton Wood elegantly, calmly, cradled that ball with such sureness and composure. When I watch it afterwards (again, and again, and again) I can't believe his poise.

Such a tiny crack of fate and time there was – such a different torrent of emotions to be unleashed if he'd lost his feet or fumbled the ball. An infinitesimal moment of decision, belief, skill and courage. It raised a roar, we learnt afterwards, from the neutral fans in the MCG bars, capturing the imagination of not just Dogs fans but football romantics (they still exist) everywhere.

Bob Murphy is being interviewed. His joy is plain to see. It's the best win *ever*, he says to Barry Hall, who, even though he played for the Swans as well as the Dogs, is not doing a very good job of looking detached and objective. Bob winks at Barry and runs joyously over to his men, his boys. He and former captain Matthew Boyd grab each other in the biggest and fiercest of bear-hugs. How must they feel, these two survivors of our 2008–10 premiership tilt? Having painfully reconciled themselves to the knowledge that a flag would elude them, now they are witnesses, tutors and leaders of this young group. They must be feeling at least the merest flicker of hope. That they're not done with yet.

I leave my fellow hoarse and exhausted Libba Sister and drive home. Bob is now on the radio, his voice still cracking with fatigue and emotion. As always, he has just the right words to capture what we've just seen. He says the match was like *Rocky IV*. Like an under-12s match, as players chased the ball up and down a boggy field. They ask him if he's given up on the dream; does he hope, still, that he might be there if this group wins a flag? Bob quotes the musician Paul Kelly, and says he just thinks about one more song.

I find the Kelly quote the next day: 'I wake up every morning and hope there's still one more tune ambling towards me down the road.'

THE TROUBLES WE'VE SEEN

Libba Sister 1, text message: 'We've been in the media all week. I've got a bad feeling. We're going to get smashed.'

Danny from Droop Street, caricature Bulldog pessimist, phone call to the Coodabeen Champions: 'I don't like it. I don't like it at all. We're being talked up everywhere. We're flavour of the month. I just know it. We're going to get smashed.'

My rambling thoughts: 'I'd like to enjoy just one week of positivity, feel happy that we're in the news for all the right reasons, and have faith in these kids.' (*And after reading the Thursday-night selections, and seeing that every tipster has selected us to win ...*) 'We're going to get smashed!'

Wooden spoons and club infighting. Woeful finals efforts where we looked like deer in the headlights. Captains who walked out on us: Templeton, Dempsey, Griffen. Men who won Brownlows after the Dogs had offloaded them: Brian Wilson, Bernie Quinlan, Barry Round. Battered cars around the western suburbs, with faded bumper stickers: 'Up yours Oakley!'

Stirring wins followed by miserable losses. Turning points, after which we saw more of the same. Season-defining wins that, well, didn't end up defining anything.

These are our stories as Bulldogs fans: the troubles we've seen. Danny from Droop Street makes us laugh and wince in equal measure, with his gloomy world view, his conviction that every win is just papering over the cracks, that every moment of happiness will just rub salt into the wounds when the loss comes – as it surely will.

I'd love to leave the past behind, believe in each new group that comes along, untainted by the shadows of our long history of failure. I'd love to believe that each new era of players, young men who start with such precocious confidence and innocent love of the game, are different – that they will make their own history, and so write a different story for us.

All week, even as we basked in the footy world's current infatuation with our team, we have had the niggling fear that our happiness was tainted, poisoned like Snow White's apple. Doesn't this praise and attention really only mean, as Danny is grouchily predicting, that a fall is just around the corner?

Are we 'getting ahead of ourselves'? Whatever that mysterious phrase might mean, it was certainly not something the unfashionable Bulldogs should ever contemplate. Are we 'dreaming too loud' as Ned Kelly put it? (With his Irish heritage and knack for heroic failure, I wonder: was he a Bulldog, perhaps?)

Are we rashly inviting fate by calculating the 'certain' wins that could see us as unlikely finalists – and maybe even, if the cards fall right, a top four proposition? Perhaps it would actually be a relief to stop daydreaming about Bob Murphy holding the premiership cup and return to the reassuring comfort of a pessimistic and curmudgeonly outlook.

And so begin the pre-emptive excuses, rationalisations and justifications before we play the Saints. The Dogs will be sore after their bruising, brutal encounter in the wet against the Swans. It will be deflating, after such an emotional victory, to get motivated again in a match where we are (*Oh no!*) favourites. The team selections add to my unease. Two of the stars of last week's heroics against the Swans, Lin Jong and Matthew Boyd, are both out.

The match against the Saints is billed as that of two very young, up-and-coming teams, but the reality is obscured by the Dogs' barnstorming, surprising start to the season. The Saints aren't actually as raw and green as us; they have seven players with more than 100 games under their belts. The Bulldogs outfit, with an average age of 23 years and seven months and only 43 games, will be one of the youngest, most inexperienced ever.

Still, our fears are allayed by the way the Dogs start. The fanatical forward pressure is still there, the manic ball movement as frenetic as ever. As we move into the second quarter the Dogs are right on top, becoming more and more dominant, building a lead that will be a buffer if we begin to tire.

We aren't imagining, at the half-time break, that we could lose. But our hearts are full of another kind of sorrow. Halfway through the quarter, Clay Smith, only a few games back from his second knee reconstruction, moves awkwardly and goes to ground, just in front of us. The crowd gives an awful moan as we see it, all of us rising to our feet, devastated at the thought that this kid – who is just 21 – may have suffered a knee injury for a third time. He is helped off the ground. The medical staff look grave.

A few minutes later there is delighted applause when Clay returns, and some relieved, almost embarrassed chuckles that our fears have been so misplaced. *You can't keep Clay down*, we tell each other. *The kid's tough as nails.*

When his knee buckles again ten minutes later, in the most innocuous of movements, the atmosphere in the crowd is thick with emotion. As he is wheeled off on a stretcher to who knows what future – who could blame him if he is unable to endure yet another round of gruelling, lonely rehabilitation – our cheers are ragged, from choked throats, as if we know how hollow they must seem while his tears flow.

I wonder what the injury will do to the spirit of our group. They've watched Clay for the past two years working and working to get himself back out there and playing the game he so loves. Witnessing his distress: it must surely have an impact.

Yet the Dogs start the third quarter well. Jake the Lair kicks a bomb from 50 (while pretending not to see any of his teammates in better positions, of course). We are 55 points up. It should, for even the most nervous Bulldog pessimist, be enough.

But then the rot sets in.

The tackles aren't sticking. Koby Stevens limps up and down the boundary line, grimacing with pain with every step, yet having to return to the field while we try to arrest the impact of Clay's injury. Jake the Lair leaps from behind, trying to take mark of the year (he doesn't), when there had been space to lead. Bob Murphy, who hasn't made a mistake for weeks, actually gets caught when trying to play on, such a rarity that it's a bad omen. The sure hands of The Bont suddenly resemble the butterfingers of mere mortals. Lukas Webb, whose calmness and poise were features even in last week's

Sydney cauldron, now looks every bit the 18-year-old kid he is, fumbling and hesitant.

We look tired, so tired.

The Saints snatch the lead when last week's hero, Easton Wood, slips over in a contest at the critical moment. Against Sydney his sure feet had saved the match. The footy gods love this sort of twist.

There are still three minutes to go. Not one person in the stadium thinks the Dogs can win. We are all longing for the siren, knowing our team are out on their feet.

Seven days ago the sound of the siren brought us wild jubilation, the delirium of a sweet victory. But now it brings a familiar numbness. I don't want to learn, for what seems the thousandth time, that our foreboding had been right – that pessimism, not hope, was the right emotion after all.

The players aren't sprinting off the field this week, bouncing on their toes, high on adrenaline as they get ready to sing the song. They're subdued, moving slowly and heavily. It's a poignant moment when their wounded teammate, even more slowly and heavily, comes out onto the field to join them. Clay could have hidden in the rooms and nursed his anguish, but he hobbles out. It's a sight which, for me, instantly obliterates all disappointment at the loss.

The fact that Clay is still wearing his red substitute's vest is somehow the most heartbreaking detail of all.

What will be the story of this loss? As our fans, some angry, many despairing, begin absorbing the fact that we've made history for all the wrong reasons (this being the fifth-biggest margin that a team had squandered), it is only too easy to see it as another example of some invisible, fatal flaw in our club's make-up. Was it yet another depressing example of our lack of success breeding further lack of success? Had that kernel of doubt that was in every Dogs fan's nervous mind in the build-up – that fear of 'dreaming too loud' – ground its way, slowly, insidiously, into these boys' psyches as well?

There could be another, less dramatic explanation, of course – that this is a meaningless blip in this group's story, something no one except footy historians will ever remember when and if they achieve the ultimate.

Hard though it is for we fans who have been through so much, the loss to the Saints tells us nothing about the calibre of this group. Nor does it say anything significant about the culture of our club, unless as fans we choose it to be so. It doesn't confirm that it was 'just like us' to drop this match. It doesn't mean that some sort of malevolent spirit will continue to blight us for ever and a day.

All it really says is that a young, inexperienced, fatigued bunch of kids, who've given their all for weeks and taken us with them on a magical journey, finally ran out of luck and legs. We can choose to believe that they and their coach will continue to build upon the astonishing, exhilarating improvement, and banish the idea that there is any deep and meaningful lesson about the culture and psyche of our club to be learnt.

Loss, failure and pain have been our story as fans, but they don't have to be the story of Jake Stringer, Lukas Webb, Tom Boyd or Marcus Bontempelli. Their tale is still theirs to write, with us fans clinging to their coattails in their crazy magic carpet ride. No one would deserve more than Clay Smith to recover in time to be there too. After all, when he was drafted, Clay got a tattoo across his chest. It read: *Living the dream.*

REASONS TO BELIEVE

Winter is looming. The Dogs' momentum has spluttered to a halt. The capitulation against the Saints was followed by a brave loss to the undefeated ladder leader, Fremantle, and then a poor showing against the Dees. Since our barnstorming win against Sydney, we've lost three matches in a row. There's no more talk of sneaking into the finals. The energy has leached from our fatigued young team. And as the thrill of our unexpected start to 2015 fades, I prepare myself for more familiar territory: a slide back to mediocrity, maybe even some mid-season thrashings.

It's far from uncharted territory, of course. As the sense of fun and adventure disperses, I ask myself, as I have so many times before, why it all matters and why my footy team has such a hold on me.

Because, really, the devotion of the fan to a spectacularly unsuccessful club like mine is a baffling phenomenon. It certainly can't be explained by the dull corporate lingo adopted by the AFL, whose annual report now has mystifying references to a 'customer segmentation framework', 'match-day consumer experience' and 'choice modelling to establish optimum membership product mixes'. With our Dogs lagging in virtually every key performance indicator – not to mention being sadly deficient in key deliverables, such as … well, a premiership – something else must account for the collective insanity of myself and other Bulldog fans.

Customer segmentation frameworks can't account for the fact that even though I am a supposedly mature adult, concerned in daily life with the wellbeing of refugees, social justice and other altruistic causes, I can refuse to leave the house until I locate my lucky Marcus Bontempelli badge, and can become unreasonably agitated by the actions of short, bald persons (otherwise known as umpires). Whatever it is that has seen me remaining (more or less) patiently in my seat when thrashings are inflicted, or that drives me to continue to support the Dogs through season after season of failure, it must be something deep, mysterious, inexplicable and tribal.

A documentary with the not so prophetic title *Year of the Dogs* portrayed the experience of the fans and the players during one of those familiar, wretched seasons, 1996. Much of the action was seen through the eyes of mother-and-daughter fans Pat and Jenny Hodgson. Their love and loyalty for the team is poignant. 'Poor darling boys,' Pat says after yet another hiding.

At one point we see a Western Oval training session. It's the depths of winter. The camera slowly pans back to show Pat and Jenny, decked in their scarves, huddled under an umbrella in the pouring rain. Unsurprisingly, they are the only supporters there. The players jog past in a soggy miserable-looking bunch. Pat leans over the fence to applaud them. 'And they'll get another clap,' she says defiantly, presumably to the bemused cameraman.

I can't really say why, like Pat and Jenny, I am compelled to support my club through what's been mostly 'thin'. In the leanest of seasons I've got by with the hope that, unexpectedly, there might be just one little moment to treasure, a time capsule to be stored away forever, one precious moment that is funny, silly, tragic, touching, exhilarating or uplifting.

It might be the rainy Western Oval day that Glenn Coleman broke a point post. Or searching in the *Footy Record* to find out more about this skinny 17-year-old in the number 29 guernsey, C. Grant from Daylesford, who has just kicked four goals in his first match. Doug Hawkins jostling with Dipper on the wing, where he was so dominant they named it after him. The immortal line from a frustrated fan: 'The Dogs have had more passes than Bruce Ruxton on *Mastermind*.' Todd Curley being dubbed 'The Pubic One' by a wit in the crowd.

Libba the First's final game, when he was chaired from the ground, one eye closed and blackened, the most unlikely – and yet the truest – of football heroes. That fragment of play in which an unpromising fringe player shows the intangible 'X' factor and you know he's going to make it. The night final at which, instead of the national anthem, chords of 'Highway to Hell' blared out of the sound system at the MCG.

Being there, just being there, with my club through heartaches like watching Chris Grant being robbed of a Brownlow. I wept as my favourite player, Daniel Cross, who was known not for elite skills but for fanatical and selfless courage, was chaired off the ground for the last time, unwilling and unready to retire, dumped by the club to which he could not have given more.

I sat stoically in a train carriage of Bulldogs fans which had all the solemnity of President Lincoln's funeral procession, after a 130-point annihilation (one of those shown in *Year of the Dogs*). I shared the hysteria-tinged laughter that erupted in that carriage when some droll young men broke the silence, tossing around ludicrous theories about how we would stop the carnage next week.

I watched Brad Johnson's last game, where the champ had lost his dazzling skills; he was so obviously older and slower, floundering and hesitant, and was beaten badly in a contest. There was an ache in my heart, because I'd watched and followed him since he was a rosy-cheeked western-suburbs teenager beaming with pride when he was drafted to the team he had grown up supporting. And because I knew that, despite his outstanding career of 364 games, his years as our captain, his regular inclusion as an All-Australian, the words 'premiership player' would now never appear in any list of Brad Johnson's accolades.

And it means something, that the best moments of footy are shared. Because as every interstate match proves all too well, the 'match day consumer experience' cannot be the same without our combined noise, anticipation, sorrow and joy, our nerves all jangling at the same time in a close match, our unified groans of despair, our collective intake of breath as a player does something crazy-brave, our voices lifted together in our tribal song. There are the little vignettes we share with the strangers who sit around us, the exchanges of rueful smiles, grimaces and head shakes at fluffed opportunities, the gasps as an injury happens, the joy when from nowhere we snatch a game.

I like knowing that echoes of the playing generations that have gone before still whisper around the current crop of players. While we watch Luke Dahlhaus bustling around the ground in his number six, we remember Brad Johnson and, further back, though I never saw him play, the nuggetty Charlie Sutton. Bob Murphy soars for a mark in his number two guernsey and a vague memory stirs: Merv Hobbs wearing the same number, in an iconic poster that graced every western-suburbs fish-and-chip shop.

We look back at black-and-white photos of the early crowds at the Western Oval and marvel at some of the quaint differences: the men in their hats and suits, some fearsome-looking matriarchs with umbrellas that you knew they were itching to wield on hapless opposition fans. Yet I wonder how much has really changed, even when I follow my club's deeds on Twitter or wrestle with a temperamental app when they're playing thousands of kilometres away.

But really, as I put aside the fruitless questions of why it all matters, reach for my lucky scarf and Bonti badge, and head off each week to meet my fellow Libba Sister, I know we're just the next links in the long and mysterious chain of fans of the Footscray Football Club.

CEDE NULLIS

I'm heading to our match against GWS feeling apprehensive. And it's not just because, after some indifferent recent form, we badly need the four points.

I have a childish, spiteful dislike of the Giants. I'm rattled by pretty much everything they represent: another step into a brave new world of football that many of us never really wanted, a world that's often threatened to leave my Bulldogs behind.

My paranoia about the lengths to which the AFL would stoop in order to ensure the Acronyms' success was such that I initially misread our team selections and was outraged that Stewart Crameri was not in the team because he had been abducted! (An adductor muscle strain turned out to be the more prosaic explanation. But still. It could have happened.)

Greater Western Sydney entered the competition in 2012. They wear orange and charcoal, and are called the Giants; their mascot is a character called G-Man. (I don't get it either.) Their website says they have four core values: innovation, integrity, inclusion and aspiration. That's okay if you like that sort of thing, I guess.

GWS have been granted endless concessions, allowed to skim off the cream of young talent of the land, and gifted millions of dollars. Along with Gold Coast, in their outfits that are reminiscent (appropriately) of Ronald McDonald, the path to success of these 'franchises' isn't a noble, heartwarming story to be admired and celebrated. It's simply what you'd reasonably expect, given the advantages they've been granted. Their inevitable success will be a return on investment, not a fairytale.

I can't even conceptualise them as a 'club' – a warm, welcoming home to the usual range of crusty and eccentric characters, like the obligatory cranky old boot-studder with a heart of gold, and fans who will passionately debate for hours exactly what went wrong in that last match – or another long-forgotten one from decades ago. Fans who can feel physically sick when their lead is at risk in the last quarter, people who get the joke when someone calls out, 'You're a disgrace to Groenewegen's jumper!'

Much though I may loathe and resent our Victorian rivals and feel jealous of their success, I can recognise in them kindred spirits whose loyalty and passion have been shaped around a past that stands for something. (Yes, even Collingwood, Carlton, Richmond and Essendon have known pain, defeats and humiliation.) These teams still have the silent but ghostly aura of old tribal loyalties and neighbourhood animosities. Trophies, team records in copperplate handwriting, sepia photos of players with exotic waxed moustaches and lace-up guernseys, lockers with names engraved of players long gone but still remembered.

Driving to collect my sister, I pause at the lights, near the clock above what used to be the Kinnears rope factory in Ballarat

Road. It mightn't be as iconic as the Skipping Girl Vinegar sign (how come western-suburbs landmarks are never as celebrated?) but it used to be clearly visible from most parts of the flat Footscray landscape, including my grandparents' house. It's been a while since Kinnears actually manufactured any rope. The deserted site is, I hear, earmarked for a boutique housing development.

When the VFL tried to boot Footscray out of the competition in 1989, one of the many letters and donations came from a whip-around among the Kinnears factory workers. They raised $200. They were among many, many fans who just refused to let the club die.

I drive around the corner, and there's the Whitten Oval itself. The team that first called itself Footscray in the 1870s soon changed its name to the Prince Imperials. Bizarrely, this was to honour the French heir to the throne. Perhaps it was an early identification with heroic failure – the prince had come to a gruesome end, disembowelled at the hands of Zulu warriors. Soon afterwards, club history recites that 'with a lack of players and membership commitment, a crisis meeting was held at the Royal Hotel to decide whether the club would continue'. Bloody hell! Even back in 1882 we were in strife. The Prince Imperials name was ditched and the Footscray Football Club lurched back from the brink for the first time. Our motto is dignified and simple: *Cede Nullis*, or 'Yield to None'.

There is another reason my mood is subdued as we take our seats to watch the former Prince Imperials at Docklands. My ill-feeling towards GWS isn't just because I fear the prospect that, sooner rather than later, the MCG will be decked out in orange and charcoal on grand final day (though that is the stuff of nightmares). It's personal, visceral, because today, for the first time since his defection, Ryan Griffen will take the field against us. How the crowd will respond to him has been a talking point all week, with a fierce debate going on. To boo or not to boo; that is the emotional and sometimes bitter question.

There is no way I want to be part of an angry, baying mob, hurling vicious insults at our former captain. I think of Martin Flanagan, who once said, after standing near an embittered and vitriolic Collingwood supporter, 'I knew he was actually telling the story of his own life.' Yet towards Griffen my feelings are complex. I feel sadness that something went so awry for him, that by all accounts he lost his love for the game that he played so brilliantly, yet I also feel profound disappointment and dis-illusionment at the timing and manner of his departure.

I wonder, too, how our players will feel about confronting Griffen in his new colours. Is it just business as usual for them, no different from a work colleague moving on to seek new opportunities? With their insiders' perspectives, maybe they feel more resigned and philosophical about Griffen's defection than the fans, for whom the news came as a devastating bombshell.

It is possible, of course, that it could work the opposite way. Our players could feel even more intensely aggrieved, because for them this was betrayal by a mate. After all, these guys quite literally bleed alongside each other. This isn't the departure of cardigan-wearing Bill from payroll who's taken up a new role with a Sydney-based branch of the company. Griffen is the bloke who led the team out each week, around whom they'd clustered before each game. A fellow sufferer in icy recovery sessions at Williamstown beach or slogging training camps in 40-degree heat. A comrade alongside them at awful moments on field when bones break or ligaments tear.

Mitch Wallis gave an interview this week in which he said that he had 'pencilled in' this game at the start of the season; that Griffen's departure had 'hurt', and he expected the encounter to have more spice than usual. Revealingly, a sanitised version of these comments soon appeared on the Dogs' website, saying only that Wally was 'looking forward' to the game as a test of how the two young lists stacked up. The more experienced media performer Matthew Boyd was then hastily rolled out to blandify the rhetoric.

Within moments of the first bounce, my questions about how our players will approach this match are answered. They are switched on, playing a high-intensity, physical, courageous style of football, harrying the Acronyms, forcing them into error and playing the game on our terms.

The passion of our players gladdens me. It is, I feel sure, no coincidence that an enormous, bone-jarring tackle just when we needed it most – when the Acronyms creep back into the game in the third quarter – is delivered by the captain who had handed the baton to Griffen, Matthew Boyd. Or that Bob Murphy celebrates his last-quarter goal with extra zest and emotion, and then follows up with an uncharacteristic physical jostle with Griffen. Or that senior players Jordan Roughead and Liam Picken commit selfless act after selfless act to push the ball forward or thwart an opposition attack.

Best on ground, with an inspirational game, is one Mitchell Wallis, who shows us that, yes, this son of a life member and former captain is a young man who cherishes our club's history and honours its meaning.

And as for the booing of Griffen – during the match it doesn't really become the issue that I'd dreaded, simply because he has a wretched afternoon and rarely touches the ball.

When the final siren goes, our players and fans alike wear their hearts on their sleeves. It is one of those memorable moments when the crowd and players come together in a feeling of oneness and belonging. I look at the expressions on the faces of Murphy and Boyd, which say this was a mission achieved and accomplished. I share their grim pride. The 'Saltwater Lads' (another early nickname) have stood tall. That horrid day when we'd apathetically capitulated in Gia's last game – well, it's not avenged, but it already feels a long time ago.

The players jog around the boundary line, touching hands with the fans. Celebrating his very first win is an awestruck, shiny-eyed third-gamer, Dale Bailey (or is it Bailey Dale? I never can remember). He looks so heartbreakingly young that I'm convinced he calls his captain Mr Murphy and his coach Mr Beveridge.

Bailey Dale's mentor is Mitch Wallis. 'He said to me, "Just put your head down and earn the respect of the boys,"' our new number 31 says earnestly in his first radio interview.

I think about his future and the journey he's about to embark upon, and wish that football will always be so simple for him. I hope he will never know moments like those of the blank-faced Ryan Griffen, who leaves the arena to boos and jeers, an exile from our club and his former brothers in arms.

A YEAR OF MIRACLES

Our rows at Docklands Stadium stand, for once, silent and empty when our team plays Port Adelaide, in a match that could well determine whether we lock in an improbable finals spot. We are at a different place of worship, celebrating the confirmation ceremony of my youngest nephew, Joel. Yes – linked to the deep well of Bulldogs-supporting pessimism is the fact that our family are Irish-Catholics. (A family friend of a similar ilk once despairingly summed up the triple disadvantage under which we labour: 'Western suburbs, Footscray supporters, Irish-Catholics. No wonder we all have chips on our shoulders!')

We sit fidgeting in the church, trying furtively to check scores on our phones and keep blasphemous language in check when we see that the Dogs are, far too quickly, three goals down. Then we have to contain urgent mutterings when we notice that the tide is turning, and quickly. The Dogs are storming over the top of Port. We aren't there when what sound like 50,000 Dogs fans ride our team home – though with three generations of my family absent, the ranks are sorely depleted.

By the final siren we are safely seated in front of a TV, scoffing party pies in Joel's honour, and watching our grand performance with delight, amazement and awe – the three emotions I'll always associate with this season. We hear the song being sung and the Bulldogs chant go up. Another chapter has been written in this year of miracles.

As I leave the celebration behind, it's not only the party pies I'm having trouble digesting. I'm trying to come to terms with our transformation from the battling, joyless grinders of 2014 to this infectiously enthusiastic group. Our football is now played in perpetual motion. It's a cross between ballet and acrobatics. There are so many moments where, after an audacious forward thrust, we gasp and look at each other. 'Did you see that? Did you really see that?'

These are heady and (because we're us) scary moments for any Bulldogs fan. We've been waiting for the bubble to burst. Protectively, we cling to talk of 'danger games' to ease the pain if – or, as we think of it, when – normality resumes. We hose down hope with recollections of some of our 'rabbit in the headlights' finals performances, our embarrassing inability to deliver on the big stage, sorrowful memories of underachievement. After all, there are plenty of statistics to draw upon to dampen our enthusiasm. We can always reach for that ultimate hope-quencher: the fact that we've appeared in only 44 finals in our 90 years in the competition, and won only 14 of them.

To believe. To hope. To rip aside the defensive, protective walls. They're the hardest thing when you've had a history like ours.

But perhaps my time under the church roof has paid off, because I find myself wanting to pause and give thanks for the delight that this most unexpected season has given us already, and cherish the reasons why we're here.

At the heart of it is Luke Beveridge, who doesn't believe in tagging and has some form of charismatic connection and feel for our club and his young charges. He has the most abundant locks in the business and wears his heart on his sleeve, high-fiving the crowd as he walks among them.

Every week we say his selection tactics make no sense, and every week his bold moves and faith in the young brigade pay off. He is reputed to skateboard to and from the Whitten Oval, he surfs on the weekend, and he tells 'dad jokes' to the players to relax them before a game. We hear that he's dubbed our style 'Men of Mayhem'. It's so delectably far away from the drab, Ross Lyon–style talk of processes and structures.

The transformation of our team, overseen by 'Bevo Our Saviour' (the nickname started as a joke but now I'm not so sure) is nowhere more apparent than in the rejuvenation of Matthew Boyd. Because recently, our number five took a hanger. A spectacular, sensational, bona fide speckie. A thing of beauty. Right in front of us. It may have been his first ever; in fact, I think it almost certainly was. But the way he's playing, you wouldn't bet on it being his last.

Matthew Boyd, the former Frankston reserves player who's based his game on pure work ethic and a fanatical commitment to training rather than the fancy stuff, was once pigeonholed as a player who could accumulate 40 possessions a week but wouldn't hurt the opposition with any of them. Now, as a reinvented back-man, his disposal efficiency statistics apparently rival Murph's.

Best of all, I loved hearing that Bevo recently confronted the team and asked whether anyone was daydreaming about finals. No one dared own up to the cardinal footy sin of 'getting ahead of yourself'. But afterwards, Matthew Boyd, a 32-year-old with an endearingly stern countenance, admitted he might just have been fibbing.

The other standout in our year of miracles is The Bont. He's at the other end of the age and career spectrum from Boyd, and he has brought so much excitement, magic and sheer entertainment to our club. He's one of those players who the crowd makes a special sound for. A new generation of kids is getting starry-eyed about football again, and number four badges are selling like hotcakes. Stephanie calls his influence 'The Bont factor'. She runs down to the fence at the end of each game, hoping to get a word with him. I should be past such adulation, of course, but for some reason one day when I bought her a new badge, one bearing the name Marcus Bontempelli also found its way into my handbag. Now it's pinned proudly to my scarf each week.

The 2015 season has featured other excitement machines too. Whenever these players get the ball, our fans begin to stir in delicious anticipation and hope of what might come next. It could be Jason Johannisen careering through the middle on one of his exhilarating runs. Or Jake the Lair bustling towards the ball, making the impossible look simple and then celebrating with his trademark strut. It could be Easton Wood's soaring marks, dazzling athleticism and remarkable bravery, or Bob Murphy's feather-light sidestep, followed by a beautifully weighted 50-metre pass on his wrong side. It could even be Matthew Boyd taking a screamer. But I don't think anyone but Matt saw that one coming.

Last week, some members from the dwindling ranks of our solitary 1954 premiership team were in the rooms and met Luke Beveridge after our 97-point win against Melbourne – the team they comprehensively defeated in that grand final so many years ago. Our team were wearing black armbands that day to honour the memory of that brilliant young 'excitement machine' among the '54 legends, E.J. Whitten. It was a mark of respect for the Bulldogs fans who have passed away this year too. There were some wry smiles at this announcement. So many of us have wondered, as the years drag by, if we will see the Dogs win a flag in our lifetimes.

The vision of the premiership heroes makes me melancholy. And then strangely hopeful. Wasn't it the Boston Red Sox who waited 86 years between World Series championships, breaking something called (perplexingly) 'The Curse of the Bambino' in the process? Anything, I tell myself, really can happen – even a Matthew Boyd speckie.

SALTY AND GRUMPY

When my oldest son was in Grade Prep I got a phone call from the school asking me to collect him as he was feeling unwell. I rushed to his classroom, fearing a major emergency. But as we walked back to the car, he was showing no particular signs of illness, and he explained to me that he'd decided to opt out of school for the day because he was feeling 'salty and grumpy'.

This splendid description has become a family catchphrase for otherwise inexplicable ennui and crankiness. And it is this condition to which I succumb as the siren sounds in Brisbane and the Dogs are defeated by the lowly Lions, in the last match of the 2015 season.

Of course, the outcome doesn't really matter. Our spot in the finals is secure. With nothing on the line, self-preservation has clearly kicked in and the Dogs were, understandably, intent on playing 'bruise-free' footy. But I stomp around a little too loudly in the kitchen post-match, muttering the names of offenders whose efforts had not been to my satisfaction.

Was it too much to ask for the Dogs to soothe our pre-finals nerves by a straightforward, effortless romp in the park to finish off this amazing season? I'd even have taken a pedestrian four-goal win. Instead, the loss feels like a sneering, ill-timed interjection or a cunningly placed roadblock, especially once it becomes clear that we would be playing That Certain Team From South Australia. (Like a member of some superstitious tribe, I don't even want to name our enemies from preliminary finals past.) And the match will be at the MCG, no less. I seem to recall it didn't turn out too well there several times in the past.

But I know in my heart the real reason for my over-the-top reaction to the loss. It's been such fun this season, riding the wave, joyously accepting our unexpected, amazing progress. Now, suddenly, unexpectedly, it all matters again. Making the finals means the Dogs have crossed a line. We're on the threshold, now, of the Land of Hope and (could it be?) premiership Glory.

There was, after all, a comfort in low expectations, in saying: 'All I expect from this year is seeing the kids develop.' Chronic failure might hurt, but it's familiar, comfortable, cosy-slippers stuff. Now it feels like we're about to jump out of a plane, not knowing where (and indeed whether) our parachute is going to land. And a crash-landing means that dreadful fist-in-the-stomach pain that is finals defeat.

And yet, for eight sides in the competition, there will be no wild leap out of a plane. Their seasons are over. But Our Dogs are not one of those teams. Not this year.

Other clubs are announcing the retirements, forced or otherwise, of players no longer required. Champs who carried the Geelong fans to the ecstasy of three flags are given their marching orders; they're farewelled with dignity, but none of them feels it's really 'their time'.

Daniel Cross ends his career at Melbourne with yet another suicidal 'eyes-on-the-ball' act of reckless courage; he gets carried off by stretcher. You know for certain that Crossy would most definitely not have felt it was 'his time'. His best mate, Matthew Boyd, stands in the Melbourne race, applauding him off the field, even though the warrior now wears another team's colours. Boydy will be playing in September again.

An athletic but spindly teenager (we probably still called him Marcus back then) took over Crossy's revered number four guernsey. I've heard that, minutes before the final siren of our match against Port, The Bont delivered an enormous crunching tackle, even though we were 10 goals up. Among the delighted crowd who rose to their feet to applaud this act of desperation was a rosy-cheeked man with a receding hairline: our games record-holder, Brad Johnson, our skipper the last time we played in September, when we lost our third preliminary final in a row and Brad's storied career came to a close.

Spring is in the air, and finals talk is all around. And this year Dogs fans aren't on the sidelines: we're among the conversation, hungry for every snippet of news about our team, debating possible selections. I see news footage of Dogs fans queuing up overnight in the cold and rain to secure their finals tickets – this for a match where you could probably walk up and get tickets an hour before. Seeing their dedication, the steadfastness of their hope and loyalty, brings on that mix of laughter and tears that this crazy business of being a supporter evokes in me so often.

There's no use feigning the salties and grumpies. We're going to see our kids, who've given us this year of boundless fun, running out onto the G. Jake the Lair and The Bont will be under the lights on the big stage. The coin will be tossed by Murph, the man who was born to be our captain. We'll shout ourselves hoarse in the massive roar that can only happen when the ball is bounced for the first time in a final. We'll be with them for all the excitement, fear, terror and joy of whatever's to come on the magic carpet ride.

DON'T DREAM, IT'S OVER

I'd forgotten how excruciating the wait before a final can be. The day drags. My emotions are all over the place. Embracing the moment. Terrified of the moment.

Finals polarise your feelings. It's like a pendulum that swings wildly from one extreme to the other. The middle ground – of hoping for an honourable performance, whether a win or loss – just doesn't cut it when there's so much at stake.

The songs on my iPod are imbued with superstitious meaning, messages from the universe. Crowded House warns me: 'Hey now, hey now, don't dream it's over.' (I guess whether or not there's a comma after the word 'dream' makes all the difference to how you interpret that one.) Then I hear a delicate melody from The Smiths, patron saints of depressives everywhere: 'Please, please, please, let me get what I want. Lord knows, it would be the first time ...'

It's a beautiful still evening when we arrive at the G. I get a message from a Richmond-supporting friend: 'We believe in fairytales – enjoy the starry night, Bulldogs, a new beginning.'

There's that stirring ripple through the crowd: our team are about to run onto the ground. An electric current seems to hit me as the wave of sound lifts us all from our seats. There's something about these kids, something about how they've gone about their year, that can't be resisted, that has made us prouder than I can ever remember. My heart is full as I watch them burst through the banner.

Dogs teams of the past have had an embarrassing tendency to freeze in the first few minutes of finals, failing to adjust to the heightened tempo and intensity. Too often those teams were already out of the contest by quarter time. It's not the case tonight: our start is dazzling, frenetic and yet still clean and skilled. We rattle on the goals so quickly that perhaps we even stun ourselves. In the half-second in which the fleeting thought arises that this could be a rout, the Crows regroup with chilling efficiency. They come at us with precise footy and lead at quarter time.

And so begins an epic. I'll never watch it again, and there are long snatches of the game I later can't recall, because there is never a lull, never a chance to ponder the rhythms or tactics of the match, just helter-skelter footy from end to end.

In the third quarter The Bont marks 30 metres out from goal. Bulldogs crowds are so often introverted and subdued by our well-founded fear of what can happen to those who get too big for their boots, but this mark is greeted by the most extraordinary, spine-chilling chant for an individual I've ever heard our fans produce. 'Bonti! Bonti! Bonti!'

We've been waiting for moments like this, moments to see this new generation, unscathed by our awful record in finals past, poised and unafraid on the big stage. The Bont, our pride and joy, will surely not miss.

The Bont misses.

Minutes later, the ball hurtles towards him again and he marks with his long arms outstretched, in almost the same spot. That miss was an aberration, surely.

The Bont misses again.

We've spent so much energy going forward, time and again. The draining misses from easy shots are piling up. We're 11 points down at three-quarter time. I'm not sure we have much left to give. But in front of 60,000 fans, the biggest crowd most of Our Boys have ever played before, they show us they still believe.

We hit the front when Jake the Lair wheels around to shoot for goal from 50 metres, after The Bont has instinctively tapped it in the direction of his fellow prodigy. The Lair and The Bont, in one passage of play! It can't get much better than this! The thunderous roar, the celebrations among the players and fans, tells me that our momentum can't be stopped.

Our momentum stops.

We need to regain the lead. A posse of Bulldogs breaks through the defensive lines and charges together through the middle. Only a sloppy, wayward disposal can thwart an inevitable goal.

A sloppy, wayward handball thwarts an inevitable goal.

There are a couple of minutes left but the Dogs are done. We're out of the 2015 finals race. And there's only room for one simple and far too familiar emotion right now: pain. It's too early yet for consolation, for fierce pride in our spirited performance, and this year of miracles. That will come later. Right now, it's too raw to have perspective as that song, the anthem of our conquerors in The Preliminary Final that Must Not Be Named and The Other Preliminary Final that Wasn't Really Very Good Either, blares out. Again.

Stephanie is crying as only 11-year-olds can when their hearts are broken. She's too young to know that this heartache and disappointment was not the opposite of the joy of winning, but part of the spectrum. That the emotion that lifted us out of our seats when Jake kicked the freakish goal that put us in front can't be separated from the horrified, heads-in-hands anguish we felt when the Crows too quickly hit back.

We start that slow, losing trudge up the MCG stairs. Two Bulldogs fans alongside us, men in their thirties, notice Stephanie's tears. 'Ah, darlin'! We weren't even meant to be here – it's just not our time yet,' says one.

'Twenty-sixteen. You wait. That will be it. That will be our year,' consoles the other.

She gives a weak smile, a response to their warmth and kindness as much as their words.

We head out into the cooler air, away from the thudding noise inside the arena. Stephanie is starting to absorb what the men were saying, and talking herself back around to hope. 'Look at where we've come from. We were 14th. We didn't even have a coach, or a captain. Or a CEO,' she adds, as though this was the most diabolical aspect of our infamous October 2014. A moment later, she says bleakly: 'It's just not fair.'

There isn't very much to say to that. As I wonder if our fate will ever be different, a line from one of Springsteen's aching odes to disappointment and shattered hopes echoes in my head. *Is a dream a lie if it don't come true?*

In the car on the way home, conversation comes in fits and starts. We're slowly, painfully making sense of it. How we lost, why we lost.

Stephanie has a new take on the outcome. 'We only won seven games last year, and this year we've won 14.' A moment later: 'I'm glad we lost today. It would be worse to lose in a preliminary final. Because then we would have had our hopes up more.'

We can't help but laugh. 'Defensive pessimism,' I say.

Stephanie is puzzled by the term.

'It means being a Bulldogs fan,' explains my sister.

No Bulldogs fan after a loss like this can draw consolation from the past and put the match into its correct perspective, as a stepping-stone along the way to inevitable improvement and success. We can never view the misses and the wasted chances without the ghosts of other such moments haunting our perceptions.

In the aftermath, many fans, in their anguish at the loss of a game where we dominated every statistic, can't help but see the parade of squandered opportunities as another episode in a history of failure. They draw an unbroken line from this loss back to the great chokes of the boys of '97 and '98, and too many other years. They see the misses, the lack of composure at key moments, as a soul-destroying repetition of our inability to deliver when it counts.

They fear that this bright, new generation is already somehow tainted, that our past can never be escaped. That as they hear again and again the stories of failure, our uber-talented youngsters become destined to repeat the mistakes that cost their predecessors in our colours a flag or maybe even two.

I don't buy it. Or maybe – for once – I just simply choose not to buy it. I don't want to burden Marcus Bontempelli with that heavy history of disappointment. I prefer to think of his seven clearances, his 12 contested possessions, his seven 'one-percenters' in his extraordinary finals debut. I don't want to think of Lachie Hunter's disastrous, clumsy final handball that might have cost us the match, but the 28 times this formerly flighty and inconsistent 20-year-old drove us forward, the thousands of metres his young legs ran to keep us in the contest.

Maybe we've got no choice but to talk ourselves around, like Stephanie, to resilience and hope. Otherwise, we're conceding that our dream really is the 'lie that don't come true'. I'm hooked on hope now, remembering that unbelievable Bonti chant. I need and want to believe that we will hear it again, on a much bigger occasion, one day very soon.

2016

THE RIDE

'We've got to be there at the end. Because who knows what might happen?'

Luke Beveridge addresses his injury-riddled troops, Round 19

AN AMBUSH

Each year, during October, I keep an eye out for any unexpected news items concerning my football team – an announcement that we've been merged out of existence, for example (1989), or that our captain would rather ... well, not be (2014). But from that point on, in the twilight world called the off-season, I develop a serene, detached perspective.

I reach the philosophical realisation that having my well-being tied to the deeds of 22 blokes – not to mention three oh-so-fallible umpires, the fickle bounce of a Sherrin, and lam-entable decisions by players to handpass too high in the dying moments of a winnable final – is far from ideal. I have only a passing interest in the draft, and avoid any mention of trade week. It's far too pragmatic and ruthless for my sensibilities.

I'll fess up to the odd moment of deranged fury if I spot people wearing 'three-peat' T-shirts, and agitated moments when I wake from a clammy nightmare, still haunted by some of the Crows' Houdini-like efforts in the 2015 elimination final, muttering, 'But who's on Eddie Betts?'

But apart from such understandable lapses, I develop something approaching tranquillity. In fact, I hadn't even got around to watching the video that our club had compiled called *The Ride*, which chronicled the highs and lows of our unexpectedly glorious 2015 season. That's how zen I was.

And then, two weeks ago, I did. And my pretence of tranquillity was smashed to smithereens. I became so excitable, reliving our Year of Miracles, that I began firing off feverish texts to unsuspecting family members: 'This is OUR year! We have the team to win a flag NOW! I can feel it!' I may have even strayed into triple-exclamation-mark territory.

My equilibrium was, you could say, seriously disturbed. And then, just as quickly, I plunged into terror. Because to Bulldogs fans there's nothing more scary and threatening than that ominous, detestable, four-letter word: hope. After all, our 2015 'ride' actually ended with yet another finals loss to Adelaide, not with improbable premiership glory.

The crazy emotions that *The Ride* had stirred up float back to me as I make my way to our Round 1 match of the 2016 season, against Fremantle. It is a trip that takes a lot longer than usual as I'm driving in from Lorne, where I've spent the Easter weekend. Any doubt about whether I'd interrupt my holiday to make the two-hour trek was banished on the Thursday before, when I received a personal – yes, directed at me alone – text message from Bob Murphy. Remarkably, Bob had taken time out from training, boring team meetings and whiteboard strategising about how we would bamboozle Fremantle to implore my presence. And if Bob said he needed me there, who was I to argue?

It's a beautiful mellow morning to drive the Great Ocean Road, the surfers are out, and dogs and young families are frolicking along the beach. But my thoughts are dragged back to 2015. I have a secret fear that 2016 simply can't be as much fun, now that we expect more – now that making the finals is an expectation, not a preposterous fantasy. Maybe last year we took the competition by surprise; maybe our exhilarating but high-energy football can't be sustained for a second season. A wily fox like Fremantle's coach, Ross Lyon, has surely been plotting and scheming all summer, devising ways to dismantle our game plan. When he was at St Kilda his dour and grimly defensive coaching methods, with their emphasis on structures and processes, had so often brought us undone.

As the miles of the Great Ocean Road slip by, my daydreaming continues. I remember that Our Boys, with Luke 'The Plantagenet' Beveridge beside them (I can't believe nobody but me has commented on this uncanny resemblance), had ridden this way during summer on a training camp. Fetchingly attired in red, white and blue lycra (some, it must be said, less fetchingly than others), they'd sweated their way up and down those scenic but demanding hills. While we fans lazed through the summer months, our team was building the strength to sustain them for the gut-running that lay ahead, so they could make those extra steps and will themselves to another contest, to be stronger and fitter when gruelling last quarters had to be won. Preparing for season 2016 and the new ride that lies ahead – for all of us.

*

By the 14-second mark of the first quarter, when the Dogs storm forward and hit the scoreboard, my pre-emptive pessimism already seems ridiculous. In fact, Our Boys explode into Round 1 as though they've been fired onto the Docklands arena from a cannon.

In the almost stunned moments of the quarter-time break, after a seven-goals-to-none blitz, scenes from *The Ride* are back in my thoughts again. I remember Bob recounting the words of his new coach just before a 2015 practice match. Bevo had warned his fresh-faced charges what to expect. 'There's going to be an ambush,' he said. A theatrical, dramatic pause. 'And that ambush is going to be us.'

The things I'd fretted about – whether we could recapture our freewheeling, devil-may-care style, and the follow-up fear (I always have a few stashed away) about whether this would have to be curbed if we are to take the next step – are being answered in compelling style.

Easton Wood still flies for – and brings down – stupendously acrobatic, fearless marks, yet he doesn't let his opponents have a sniff either. His fellow defenders cruise effortlessly forward time and again. Shane Biggs and Jason Johannisen rack up so many possessions and make it look like so much fun that a rather startled Dale Morris finds himself caught in their slipstream, charging towards goal and launching a wobbly shot. If it had been a goal, the tide of affection towards our most selfless and unobtrusive champion would have surely had even Ross 'The Process' Lyon on his feet and applauding. (Maybe.)

The 2016 Bont is stronger yet just as graceful and creative. The underrated Jackson Macrae sets up so much of the blitz with his deft little touches. 'Celeb' Daniel uncannily makes something of nothing every time he goes near it. (Last year our diminutive, helmet-clad player in the number 35 guernsey was nicknamed

The Wee Man. The Libba Sisters realised, however, that we were in no position to cast stones. He's now known within our family ranks as 'Celeb', after my sister-in-law misread his name.) And the guy who missed all the 2015 fun, Libba the Second, plays like a man who knows that footy mortality can come quicker than you think. The roar of emotion from the crowd when he kicks a goal on his wrong foot within minutes of the start could even have brought a smile to the face of Ross The Process. (Perhaps.)

There is another player who features prominently. He wears, like an increasing number of awestruck young fans, the number nine.

Our somewhat introverted fans often, I think, have a fear of the cult of personality. We have a cringing 'stop that' reaction when the media gushes over Jake Stringer's prodigious, Ablett-like talents. We're embarrassed when Brian Taylor shrieks that he's 'The Package'. (I still prefer to call him The Lair.) But you can feel a ripple of amazement and then incredulous laughter when, in one moment, Jake launches himself to the heavens to attempt to steal Mark of the Year from Easton, and in the next half-second soccers a goal, with his left foot, past three flatfooted opponents. He finishes the game with five goals.

Our coach fronts the media after a win that has made that four-letter word creep stealthily back into our hearts. There is naturally little talk of 'the process' from our Plantagenet-lookalike, lycra-wearing, Men-of-Mayhem-creating coach. The media pack instead hear this pronouncement: 'We need to be good in the phone box and we need to be good in the TARDIS. We were good in both today.'

The TARDIS stands for 'Time and Relative Dimension in Space'; it's the police box Dr Who uses to travel instantaneously through time and space. Or perhaps Bevo means the millisecond in which Libba squirts out a handball, or the fraction of a blink in which The Bont blind-turns past an opponent, or when Bob, just for the fun of it, launches a 50-metre switch-kick across the ground to Easton Wood running at full tilt. Or when Jake the Lair sees a goal where none should exist.

It is the moment that I know – or maybe I decide, for footy is all about faith – that the 2016 ride is going to sweep me along again, and that I'll need to hang on for dear life in its irrepressible wake.

WHAT BECOMES OF
THE BROKEN-HEARTED?

It's one of the legacies of barracking for a not-so-successful team: ghosts are always hovering. Their whispering presence may explain the gnawing anxiety that I can't shake before we take on the Saints. Because the Saints and Bulldogs are fellow travellers on the highway of disappointment. Our clubs are far and away the two worst performed of the Victorian-based clubs. All that's up for grabs is that timeless question: who deserves the ignominious title of Worst Team Ever?

As each team has claimed just one premiership, this debate must focus on other measures. Should one rate the Saints' superior collection of wooden spoons as the best indicator of failure? They have 26, whereas we have a mere four. (However, I contend that this is an unfair measure as they've been in the competition longer.) Perhaps grand final appearances would be a fairer yardstick: only two for the Dogs, a more respectable seven for the Saints.

In 1997 this deadlock of non-achievement was set to be broken. With both teams in preliminary finals, all was in place for a meeting of the perennial under-achievers: the ultimate tear-jerker grand final, from which at least one of the lovable losers would emerge as premier. Like the fabled rivalry between Harry Potter and Voldemort, only one could emerge alive. The Dogs failed to keep their date with destiny (yep, the Preliminary Final that Must Not Be Named); the Saints at least played their part by making the grand final, but a certain South Australian team overran them. (I'm not bitter.)

More recently, the Saints twice stood in the way of us reaching only our third ever grand final berth. Ross Lyon's coaching style was a fortress we were unable to conquer. He, and they, thwarted us in consecutive preliminary finals in 2009 and '10. The first of these encounters was a grinding, intense slog. There were critical umpiring decisions so baffling that *The Age* devoted a whole page the following day to analysing them. (Not that the Bulldog faithful needed such analysis; we'd speedily concluded that all of them were wrong.)

The match, everyone said, was thrilling and enthralling. A classic. I didn't leave the MCG with the churning embarrassment of the '97 and '98 shockers. I declared myself proud, claimed to be satisfied with the Dogs' undoubted bravery and desire to win. They had given their all. There was no shame in this one. But I really didn't want to think too much about why we kept losing these close finals.

In 2010 not even our most one-eyed fan could blame the officiating. The Dogs were simply cooked: our team had limped into the finals, beset by injury and illness – we were fortunate, really, to have made it into the preliminary after somehow coming off the canvas in the previous week's final against the Swans. Our era was over, our deficiencies on display, the core of our team ageing. It was painfully apparent that either Rodney Eade's game style or the personnel at hand had proven inadequate in the most intense battles, winning us only three of the nine finals in which we competed during that period. We knew hard times were about to come. In 2011–14, they duly arrived.

The Saints, after easily disposing of us, went on to play Collingwood in the 2010 grand final. Only one famously wayward bounce prevented them from being premiers that year. The match was drawn; they lost the replay.

Football moves so quickly that there are few survivors from the 2009 epic. But one of them is the evergreen Saints captain, Nick Riewoldt, who's playing his 300th match. We've reason to fear the big, blond, athletic champion. So often he has applied the blowtorch against us, marking, leaping, running, finding one last effort to deny us a win.

If the emotion surrounding this milestone isn't enough to rattle me, seeing Shane McInerney walk onto the ground this evening certainly does. He was the umpire who made the famously contentious decision to award Riewoldt a free in front of goal in the '09 final. My antenna for disaster is on high alert.

As memories of that moment on the MCG grassy knoll re-emerge, a nightmare scenario for the last few seconds of tonight's match flashes before me …

The Dogs haven't played well against a Riewoldt-inspired St Kilda outfit, but are clinging to a one-point lead. The Saints launch an attack, via a chain of handpasses from our fatigued and flatfooted forward line. Men in red, white and black surge along the wing: Steven Milne, Lenny Hayes, Robert Harvey, Darrel Baldock. (Clearly my fevered imaginings won't allow facts to intervene.) *One of them – it could even be Barry Breen – kicks it towards*

Riewoldt, who is one-out in the forward line. Somehow, only Caleb Daniel has ended up remotely near him. 'Celeb' charges bravely towards the spiralling ball. He's ten metres in front of Riewoldt and sprints further in front of him to mark the ball cleanly, just as the siren sounds. Our ecstatic celebrations falter. Instead there is a bewildered silence. Yes, Shane McInerney is reaching for his whistle. He rules that Celeb has somehow 'chopped the arms' of the 193-centimetre giant, and awards Riewoldt a free. Right. In front. Of goal.

I blink, shake my head and realise that while this far-fetched scenario has been unfolding, the teams have run onto the ground. Even though I'm still a little traumatised, I join Saints and Dogs fans alike in rising to my feet to applaud Riewoldt and acknowledge his magnificent career.

The two very different champion captains, our Bob and their Nick, embrace in the middle of the ground. I realise there's a poignancy to their stories that is similar: despite his heroic efforts on his club's part, Riewoldt is playing in the knowledge that a premiership will almost certainly elude him, a scenario that Bob had almost come to accept before the 2015 ride. Harvey, Burke and Loewe sit ahead of Riewoldt in the Saints' depressing 'most games without a premiership' ladder; for Bob, the names Johnson, Grant, Hawkins, West and Smith (all but Dougie his former teammates) are a silent reminder. Ghosts of years, seasons, opportunities past.

As always, it is fortunate that the teams (and especially members of the umpiring fraternity) don't have a window into my imaginings.

The Dogs open briskly, purposefully. The Saints are trying to play an ultra-defensive style; often all the players are crammed into our half of the arena. (A ghostly echo from Ross The

Process?) It's a much more intense, suffocating and exhausting contest than last week. So much so that I don't really notice that we're pulling further and further away. We're 17 points up, then 25 up, then 38 up. And while I'm worrying that our skills are well down, I don't notice what's right in front of me. The margin keeps widening, and ultimately it's a thrashing. The emotion for Riewoldt hasn't bridged the gap in the two clubs' talent and desire; even not playing anywhere near as well as I'd like, we have the match well in our keeping.

Even though the Saints aren't actually younger or less experienced than us, our 'rebuilds' are at different stages. We're aiming for finals while they are still a work in progress. As we're singing our song, a Saints fan bellows at us – 'You're no good. It's just that we're crap!' – but there's no heat in his insult, no offence taken as the crowd begin to straggle away.

Now free of my fears, I realise that they are simply the ghosts of our past, the lack of alternative narratives available to successful clubs: of triumph from adversity, of bad times quickly turned around to glory. To our young talent – The Bont, Stringer, Hunter & co. – St Kilda are just another opponent, one to approach in workmanlike fashion, just four points along the way to what they want to achieve.

Only Matthew Boyd, Murph, Liam Picken and Dale Morris survive from those who came so close in 2009. Riewoldt's opponent on that long-ago night, and the instigator of the infamous bump, Brian Lake, is now a retired triple premiership player with the Hawks, and a Norm Smith medallist. Two of our best players that night – so far away and yet still so near – were Callan Ward and Ryan Griffen. They both now wear orange.

But our Dogs' attacking, audacious, devil-may-care approach is the talk of the footy world. Time has marched relentlessly on, and we're proudly perched on top of the ladder after Round 2, 2016.

MOMENTS

I've always been a devotee of the novels of Thomas Hardy. And perhaps it's a bit eccentric, but I'd long ago formed the theory that the great but gloomy Victorian novelist was somehow writing the script of the Western Bulldogs' fortunes. Indeed, of the Footscray Football Club before them. He may have even been pulling the levers for the Prince Imperials way back in the 1880s, for all I know.

Hardy is the author of novels such as *Tess of the D'Urbervilles* and (this was the clincher in confirming the link between a British novelist and the fate of an Australian rules football team) *Far from the Madding Crowd*.

My line of thinking goes like this: Ole Tom – though around any self-respecting footy club he'd be known as Thommo – specialises in ponderous coincidences. A sense of impending doom hovers relentlessly. Even when a character appears to be on the brink of happiness, Ole Tom pulls out a few contrived and heavy-handed plot twists – an overheard conversation, a letter slipped under a door, an inexplicable decision by a goal umpire, for example – all designed to ensure the continued misery of his characters.

Truth be told, Ole Tom can lay it on a bit thick. One of his characters, Jude the Obscure, is described as 'the sort of man who was bound to ache a good deal before the fall of the curtain upon his unnecessary life should signify that all was well with him again'. That can mean only one thing. Jude the Obscure was definitely one of the anguished fans among the Bulldogs crowd in 1997 when Jarman kicked those goals in The Preliminary Final that Must Not Be Named.

I reach for the 'Thomas Hardy Is Directing Our Future' theory after Round 3 because, with only a minute to go, the Dogs are leading the Hawks. Just as a stirring victory is in sight, Ole Tom ratchets up the tension.

Our beloved captain, Bob Murphy – the very best of people, exemplifying loyalty and something pure, quixotic and joyful in footy, perched on 295 games and within touching distance of the flag that almost all of the footy world badly wants for him – crumples to the deck in agony. Yep, Ole Tom is orchestrating the plot for sure; only he would extract a further masochistic pleasure in deciding that the awful sight of Bob writhing in pain on the turf wasn't sufficient. We had to lose the match as well to grind the cheerless message home.

We've all been looking forward so much to this match, the chance to measure ourselves against the yardstick that is the Three-Peaters. The answer in the first quarter is definitely not what we have been looking for. The Dogs look overawed and out of place on the big stage. As the Hawks move the ball around with clinical precision, I am wishing I hadn't read a statistic that morning stating that it's been six years since we've beaten the

Hawks. Remarkably, only four of our blokes out there today have ever played in a winning team against the brown and gold.

Our effervescent energy and quick ball moment are easily shut down by the Hawks. They are untroubled by the intense pressure we're attempting to apply. An amazing 14 of them, compared to our measly five, have played more than 100 games. Their hands haven't turned into concrete mitts like those of our blokes have; they have time and space, while our error-prone Dogs are flatfooted, slow and reactive.

As the siren sounds to end the first quarter there is a murmur in the Bulldogs crowd. A sigh of disappointment, which quickly shifts to the usual resigned fatalism. But we sit close to where Luke Beveridge and his lieutenants make their way onto the ground. As I watch Luke pass us, a study in calm and purposeful concentration, I feel unexpected hope that he will have the answers. That the game that for me looks like a shapeless mass of blunders and errors is unfolding before his eyes as a series of problems that can and will be solved. In Bevo, it seems, we really should trust.

There isn't an immediate turnaround in the second quarter; in fact the Hawks extend their lead. But there are little signs: chains of play that begin to pay off, an imperceptible lift in confidence, moments when, even if they don't bring a goal, I find myself saying, 'That looks like us.' Because 'us' is becoming a recognisable style: quick hands, numbers around the ball, no shying away from the tough stuff. The goals slowly begin to come, and with them signs of verve and flair. Confidence slowly builds.

And then comes the third quarter. Later, I will wish it hadn't been forever tainted by what came after. I'd love to watch it again, free from that sickening knowledge of Bob's injury, to see our

Bulldogs – who are conceding almost two years of experience, on average – not just outplaying the Three-Peaters but, incredibly, smashing them in contested possessions by an unheard-of 58 to 29. Holding strong in tackles, fanatically attacking the ball and the man, emerging with the ball in contest after contest to drive it forward. Not the pretty or, as some have dubbed it, 'sexy' football with which some had thought we might overpower the Hawks, but a grinding, desperate, ferocious will for the contest.

At three-quarter time we are all making a tremendous racket. We are three goals up but it should be more. My nieces and nephews start the Bulldogs chant; feet are being stamped on concrete like in the Western Oval glory days. People beam at each other, strangers do high-fives, and everyone is united in pride and amazement. It's a kind of group delirium, a trance-like state. We haven't been found wanting. We haven't slid back from 2015. We aren't 'promising' or 'on the rise'; we've actually out-willed, out-bustled, outplayed the champs. What can our amazing team achieve this year? Is this our time, at last?

The Hawks aren't buying in to the euphoria. They come at us again in the fourth. We are somehow caught by surprise, stunned and a bit affronted that they haven't meekly surrendered to our burning will and passion. 'Oh?' our exhausted looking troops seem to be saying. 'We've got to do this all over again?' And so we do.

We hit the lead again. We'll hold on this time, surely, for an epic, brilliant win in this enthralling, brutal, wonderful game. But in a slow-motion scene that I can't bear to remember yet will never forget, the ball begins sailing towards the Hawks' centre half-forward spot. And somehow Bob Murphy is alone, competing against two Hawks players.

Our captain, our heartbeat, wrecks his knee in the simplest of motions. It's the second time he's done it. He is 33 years old, not far off 34.

Little collages of Bob – memories of his career, and what he's meant to us – keep flashing before me in the minutes and hours after the match, when our worst fears are confirmed. Yes, I was there in the terraces at Princes Park, when Bob played his first match, an 18-year-old, freckle-faced, gangly kid who popped up in the last minutes to kick the wobbliest of goals. I saw his brilliant 2006 season, when he played as an unconventional and undersized centre half-forward, one who relied on skills, speed and vision rather than brute strength. I was there the first time his knee buckled, that same year, beneath a massive Sav Rocca tackle at the MCG.

I remember how Bob writes letters for new players on their debuts, slipping them into their lockers. I picture the wry smile on his face as he stood with the team for the playing of the national anthem in a final in 2009 when the sound system mistakenly blared out an AC/DC track. Our whimsical, quirky Bob could see the ridiculousness of the moment.

I think of the gratitude we felt when he put his hand up to be captain in the miserable aftermath of Ryan Griffen's departure. It was such a natural and inevitable fit that we wondered why it had taken so long to happen.

I think back to all the things he talked about in *The Ride*, which was as much a chronicle of Bob's journey as that of the club he'd unexpectedly found himself leading and inspiring. There is such a sweetness to Bob, the dad who eats McDonald's with his daughter after a game, the guy who is still awestruck because one of our club legends, John Schultz, sends him an email to congratulate him after a game. I think of Chris Grant, our gentle and gracious champ, and the light in his face as he described Bob Murphy as a 'beautiful person'.

It can't – it mustn't – end this way. Not even Ole Tom could be so cruel.

After our win against Freo, Luke Beveridge had mentioned the TARDIS. As the ramifications of Bob's injury ripple towards us, I wish there was a time machine to take us back and wipe clean, forever, all the moments of Sunday's match that led to Bob trying to get around Luke Breust and spoil the ball as it spun into the Hawks' forward line. If only we could unravel those countless actions, the kicks and handballs, the good and bad decisions, the goals and points, bounces and tackles, the random ricochets of the ball off hands or shins.

If only we could undo that fateful moment on the morning of the match when Easton Wood's troublesome hamstring unexpectedly twanged, and he was ruled out of the team. If Easton had been there, in those excruciating seconds when Bob was about to go down, surely he'd have been hurtling fearlessly across the turf, ready to support and protect his captain. He'd have jumped and flown and spoilt, and we'd never have known how close we'd come to the desolation of seeing Bob go down, and the terrible fear that we may not see him out there ever again.

THOSE MOURNFUL BOB MURPHY BLUES

I've been lying low. Coughs, colds, fevers. Soaring temperatures. Bone-rattling chills and clammy sweats that come on suddenly. An ominous array of symptoms. Overlaid, of course, with the Bob Murphy Blues. A depression brought on by thinking of a year without our spiritual leader. An even worse melancholy, if the dreadful thought pokes through, that we may never see him wearing our colours again, except through tears as he is driven around in an MCG grand final motorcade.

Dear Bob. Say it ain't so.

The media, of course, have kindly advised fans and players alike to 'put Bob's catastrophe behind us'. I heard Gerard Healy pontificating about this. We should be treating Bob's injury as though it had happened to any player on our list, and just move on and be rational. Moments later I punched the dial to turn this heresy off. 'What would you expect from a footy mercenary who left his club and took the big bucks to go to Geoffrey Edelston's pink helicopter Swans?' I fumed. A bit of hyped-up, manufactured, vaguely illogical anger is, I find, a tonic when you're battling the mournful Bob Murphy Blues.

Seemingly determined to increase our suffering, the club released the next instalment of *The Ride*: a continuation of the 2015 series, the main focus of which was the parallel journeys of Bob and Luke Beveridge. Bob called him 'the coach he'd always been waiting for'. There again was that terrible slow-motion footage of Bob's injury. In the background, the faces of our devastated fans, seeing but barely believing that Bob could go down like that, at that moment. There was the emotion in Luke's voice, the rasping throat and red eyes. The footage in the inner sanctum as Luke addressed the team, confirming that the injury was exactly as bad as it looked, and telling them all to look after each other. There was Bob's daughter Frankie, looking up at him and his crutches with trusting but bewildered eyes, then reaching out to pat his sore knee.

Over the years, concocting daydreams of what it would be like if the Bulldogs made a grand final have kept me both sane and (occasionally) not very sane at all. In the grimmer days of 2013, when we were a seriously bad team, I'd begun calculating which year was feasible and realistic, but not so far into the future that Bob would not still be out there. I'd earmarked 2016 as that very year. I can hardly claim to be a soothsayer: I'd visualised us still coached by Brendan McCartney, with Ryan Griffen our valiant captain, and Bob an ageing but valuable veteran whose spot in the team was in doubt until, at the very last minute (I love a fairytale), he ran out onto the G with his boys.

Versions of this daydream have played out in my mind again and again over the decades. Of course, I've had to cross names out and insert new ones as the unsuccessful years rolled by; most recently, it was Rocket and Johnno in a tearful embrace on the MCG. Before them it was Rocket and Chris Grant holding up the cup, or Terry Wallace, Libba the First and (for some unknown reason) Matthew Croft. I've always had a soft spot for our more unfashionable players, and Crofty, ungainly but lion-hearted, was one of those guys. It's no wonder I'm feeling poorly; I feel a sort of tiredness, a sorrow and fatigue, at the thought of having to rewrite the dream yet again if it can't include Bob.

So on Saturday night, as I head to the ground for our Round 5 game against the Lions, I fear that the thrill of the 2016 ride has already dissipated. Already half a dozen first-choice players are missing from the group that jumped out of the blocks and dazzled the footy world in Round 1.

Although all our matches have been at Docklands this season, we've alternated 'home' games there with others in which we are the 'guests'. How strange it was last week, when we played Carlton, to see all that proud arrogance, the sense of money, power, privilege and entitlement that once oozed from the very Princes Park turf, stripped away. The villainous Bourgeois Blues of my youth are just another struggling Docklands tenant, and bottom four certainties. I could still muster a healthy dash of western-suburbs animosity, though, as I watched their pre-match entertainment. Weird cartoon characters, apparently representing the Blues, ran out carrying their 16 premiership cups. This appeared just a tad over the top, given their results in the past decade or so. I wish we'd parodied it: I'd have loved to see the Dancing Dogs running out brandishing our wooden spoon collection.

Now, back in our familiar seats, the result against the Lions is beyond doubt. While our lead builds, I begin reflecting on two different pairs of players: our two oldest players, Matthew Boyd and Dale Morris, and the two Boy Wonders on which our premiership dreams are built, The Bont and Jake Stringer.

Boyd and Morris have between them played 473 games for us. Yet each came to the club as rookies. Boyd's rise was the more meteoric: he came from the ranks of the Frankston seconds. Because Bob has so often beautifully articulated his premiership dream and his longing for a flag, it's easy to overlook that his two fellow senior citizens may be burning just as fiercely in their desire for the ultimate success. The three of them went through those three preliminary finals heartaches. Together they endured the plunge to mediocrity of 2011–14, the apparently certain knowledge that their flag 'window' had opened and closed.

One of the most joyous things about the 2015 Year of Miracles was seeing the effect on our three 30-somethings, whose enthusiasm seemed to be rekindled week by week. As the young beanie-clad brigade kept crashing through expectations, you could see the realisation dawn on them that it might not be over. It was worth sticking around after all. No longer did they have to resign themselves to being teachers, role models and influencers for a group whose maturity they wouldn't be around to see. Their dream was alive, and the sweeter because they had thought it dead.

Yet two weeks ago the ranks of the three stalwarts had thinned down to two. No wonder there was such terrible sorrow on Matthew Boyd's face when he saw Bob on crutches after the Hawks match; he shared with him the longest, closest and saddest of hugs.

For some reason Boyd has always been respected rather than loved by the Dogs fans. It's a fair bet that the number five guernsey and badge aren't top sellers among the Bulldogs merchandising products. But as I watch his efforts on Saturday night I'm unsure why this has been the case, and slightly ashamed of it. I watch the kilometres he covers against the Lions, the second and third efforts which belie his age; I see him willing his way into contests to help his younger teammates, and I notice that, even after all these years, he has kept improving his game. Who knew he would ever master a neat left-foot pass? He has unobtrusively slipped into the club's top 10 for games played. And I wonder afresh why we have never fully appreciated our three-time Sutton medallist, former captain and dual All-Australian, and the immensity of his efforts for our club.

I recently read that Matthew Boyd's middle name, and hence his nickname around the club, is Keith. There was apparently unbridled hilarity among his teammates when this slipped out. The affectionate hilarity of learning something endearingly daggy about an earnest class swot, I imagine.

On the eve of his recent 250th game, I had imagined the club's media folk would have had to scratch around a fair bit harder than usual to compile his highlights package. In fact, when I saw it I was delighted, and somehow touched, to see that young Matthew Boyd, wearing number 42 and a mullet that spoke to his Frankston reserves days, once had blond tips.

The footage of Matthew Keith Boyd's milestone game had a suitably no-frills caption: 'Boyd delivers in his 250th.' Jake the Lair managed just 10 possessions the same night but still got his own highlights reel with the glitzy title: 'Jake lights up Etihad.' It's not fair, to not be a lair.

Our other thirty-something, Dale Morris, is one of our best-loved players, yet I expect many opposition fans might struggle to identify him. While durability has been one of Boyd's attributes, Dale spent 18 months on the sidelines after a horrific broken leg. The Dogs' leadership group moved their meetings to his hospital bed so they could continue to include him.

The Dogs were strugglers at the time, and Dale could easily have called it quits. But there is steel inside him: the single-minded ambition and self-belief that drove him when he was a 24-year-old Werribee player who'd been constantly overlooked. He kept sending the Dogs' brains trust videos of his play until they relented. Quietly, self-effacingly, Dale has notched up over 200 games. While his efforts have doubtless stopped countless goals, he himself has managed just three in his entire career, and I can't even remember one of them.

Full appreciation of the greatness of players such as Morris and Boyd sneaks up on the fans. But from the moment that Jake Stringer and Marcus Bontempelli came to our club they were viewed as future superstars. They were the cream of their crop, elite talents seized upon by success-starved fans.

Sometimes the euphoria of the fact that these talents are ours is so overwhelming that we can't quite believe our luck. We project onto them the stories of a lifetime of Bulldogs-supporting failure and disappointment, worrying a little too much if they have a poor match or don't dominate week after week. We fear, before their careers have barely begun, that we will lose them – that other, richer clubs will target them, that we will have to watch, empty and depressed, as they take the field in other colours. Because we assume, deep down, that they won't find success with us, and will need to move on to jag that elusive premiership.

I watch Marcus Bontempelli this week. He's at the bottom of packs. His tackles are strong and courageous. I see that whenever there's a ball-up, he's one of the organisers, directing his teammates, talking, encouraging, blocking. He spends time on the forward line, an imposing sight and a nightmare match-up with his height, power and mobility.

The Bont has not yet turned 21 but is already in our leadership group; he's played 42 games and last year ranked sixth in the competition for inside 50s. He topped our Brownlow votes with 13. He's already broken countless 'youngest ever' records. He's The Bont. Our Bont.

I also watch Jake 'the Lair' Stringer. His bristling energy, the force field of his outsized personality, has seemed a little confined over the last few weeks. Three, four defenders always seem to be around him. He's actually been – and I would never have thought this was possible – down on confidence.

The ball's in our forward line – like many of our kicks in this pedestrian, ho-hum match, it's a scrappy entry. Suddenly, a steam train bearing the number nine crashes through our forward line. Lions players fall like skittles around Jake as he turns – inevitably – towards the goals. The fans begin to rise the second they see who has the ball and what his intent is. There's a special, distinctive sound reserved for some players – an appreciation of their artistry. *Ooh!* We hear it now as Jake snaps the goal. The Lair!

As we leave the ground I think again of Boyd and Morris, remembering their unflashy one-per-cent contributions in the backline, unheralded, solid, leading by example, doing the right thing time and again. The fans are never going to stir in our seats in anticipation as one of them launches a blistering run through the centre. We're not likely to chant their names as we did for The Bont in last year's final. How do Matt and Dale feel when they look down the ground and see their freakish younger teammates? I imagine them praying, hard, that their bodies will hold up for one or two more years – whatever it takes to be out there when The Bont and The Lair take over the G.

Perhaps my fantasy of a 2016 flag was just one season too soon, I muse. We've waited a long time, such a very long time; what's another year? It wouldn't be right if it didn't feature those three 30-somethings, men who've played their hearts out side by side in a miserly backline.

I decide to project my premiership fantasy forward a year. I can see Boyd, Bob and Morris exchanging a few quiet glances as the light begins to fade in the dying moments of the 2017 grand final and they know that what they've played for all these years has finally arrived.

JUST ONE OF THOSE NIGHTS

It's halfway through the last quarter in our match against the Kangaroos. We're three goals down – a far from insurmountable margin. Jordan Roughead takes a strong contested mark, only 10 metres out from goal.

As he lines up, it should be a suspenseful, dramatic moment: a kick that could put us a step closer with time still in hand, setting the scene for a barnstorming finish in which we overpower the Roos. But I feel none of the usual tension, the excruciating agony of the wait to see the goal umpire march to the line to signal a goal. You see, I'm convinced that Roughie will miss.

Which he duly does.

I'm not quite sure why I felt so pessimistic (that is, if you discount a lifetime of Bulldogs barracking – okay, I guess that's the explanation). But there had been an earlier moment where my finely tuned 'gloom and doom' meter had been activated. The Dogs had made a hesitant start in this match, which was billed as a top-of-the-table clash. We'd appeared overawed by the occasion, by the rarity of a Friday-night big-match atmosphere. But we'd clung on, always staying within reach. And there were signs of gathering momentum in the third quarter. It was still a struggle, but you sensed that just one goal, one uplifting, inspirational moment, might change the landscape completely.

The Bont looked like he would be That Man. He loped towards goal at the 50-metre mark. We leant forward in anticipation: our prodigy was about to swing around with that booming left foot and transform our stodgy efforts with a moment of sheer individual brilliance. The Bont handballed instead. The alarmed recipient was a flatfooted, overawed Bailey Dale. He looked so young that I hoped the club had obtained a note from his mum before he was allowed out so late on a Friday evening.

As the handball floated in the lightly built teenager's direction, we knew what was going to happen. We feared what was going to happen. We groaned as it happened. Dailey Bailey's 45-kilogram frame nearly snapped in half as he was tackled by some 48-year-old North Melbourne brute, and the ball crashed to earth. The sound reverberated around the ground; it was one of those pivotal moments that said it all. This was just not our night.

Our forward line, seemingly awash with glittering talent when we slammed on seven unanswered goals in the opening quarter of season 2016, has battled to put together six for the whole evening.

We are the 'away' team at Docklands for this match. North have adopted that most ridiculous of practices, a pulsating sign on the screen after each goal accompanied by a pumped-up DJ entreating their fans to 'make some noise'. Worse still, the North fans dutifully obey; like sheep rather than flesh-and-blood sup-porters, they bleat out some cheers on cue. I envisage the next step: 'Stakeholders! Please take up this unprecedented engage-ment opportunity!'

Perched on the highest level, away from our usual seats, we have a birds' eye view, which makes it harder to forgive mistakes and easier to condemn missed chances. The game's pattern unfolds far too obviously before us, leading to whimpers of anguish as a player rebounds from defence, fails to spot the unat-tended guy who's run hard to make space, and instead picks out four North players who've camped out on the wing in anticipa-tion of just such an opportunity.

From our vantage point we watch in despair as four of our defenders cannon into each other to spoil the ball, as Jake opts for speckies instead of leading into the space that we can see stretching out before him, as tired-looking players give up the chase a little too easily.

Even worse is the slow-motion view that is afforded of the dreaded run-down from behind. While we shriek like kids at a pantomime, 'Watch out – he's behind you,' one of our players (I'd rather not label the culprit) takes one too many lumbering steps forward, seemingly the only person in the entire stadium oblivious to the hot breath of a North player on his neck.

Watching this and other disasters unfold, I realise with sink-ing heart that a phenomenon which I thought had been relegated to the not-so-nostalgic Brendan McCartney era has re-emerged, just when we needed it least. Yes, what I once called the Catastro-phe Performance Index (or CPI to insiders), consisting of aimless chaotic attempts to go forward, was rearing its unloved and ugly head again.

This is not to be confused with Chaos Theory, the style implemented with such magical results since the arrival of Bevo Our Saviour. In this much more pleasing version, we hold our breath as waves of defenders stream out of the backline in kamikaze formations, shooting daredevil handpasses out ('Wait! That can't come off!') to another red, white and blue player, who launches a manoeuvre equally implausible ('Did he just do that?'), before the ball arrives in a forward line teeming with opportunities ('Wow! Go Dogs!').

That form of chaos, though, normally had Bob Murphy at its heart, with his elegant lope through the middle, or those kicks that sliced through the opposition's press. They often featured a JJ dash to connect up the red, white and blue Men of Mayhem. Their absence means we are not simply two elite ball-users and line-breakers down; it's like we're cutting and pasting less skilled men into the same frenetic game plan. Without these sublime talents, Chaos Theory just looks crazy.

For a 16-point loss to the competition ladder leader, Friday night's performance has thrown up a disproportionate amount of angst, as we grapple again with that gigantic battle between hope and pessimism, much more stark in a team so long without success. Unsurprisingly, not only the CPI, but also its usual sidekick – Flawed Long-Suffering Bulldog Thinking (which doesn't make for a very good acronym) – have materialised.

It feels far too easy to overstate the meaning of the loss, to begin the panicky internal monologue of preparing myself for the possibility that this group, too, will break my heart, like so many others have. It's a state of unnecessary gloom and doom that only fans of unsuccessful clubs can understand. I try to channel the mindset of successful club supporters, those annoying, premiership-glutted folk in brown and gold, to ward off these evil thoughts.

Flawed, long-suffering Bulldog thinking: 'Our game style has now been exposed. Other teams have worked us out. It's THE END!'

Reasonable, rational, smug, premiership-glutted Hawthorn supporter thinking: 'If even one of Bob, JJ, Tom Boyd or "Celeb" Daniel had played, the Dogs would have won. Simple as that.'

Flawed, long-suffering Bulldog thinking: 'Last year was so much more fun. We won every week! We've gone back into our shells. We don't "believe" any more.'

Reasonable, rational, smug, premiership-glutted Hawthorn supporter thinking: 'Have you forgotten the Dogs lost to St Kilda, Brisbane and Melbourne last year? The season is a marathon, not a sprint. It's about holding on to a top four spot; of course there are bumps along the way. It's how you regroup that matters.'

Flawed, long-suffering Bulldog thinking: 'We never win the big games. Our culture of failure is now affecting this promising group. There's something wrong with our very DNA!'

Reasonable, rational, smug, premiership-glutted Hawthorn supporter thinking: 'What a load of tripe. The Dogs' list is the second-youngest in the competition. They're already well ahead of where they should be, and with an incredible amount of upside. The Kangaroos are a bunch of geriatrics, three whole years older than the Dogs on average, and all their players are fit. Even playing poorly, the Dogs still had many opportunities to win the game. You can bet the rematch will be a different story.'

Flawed, long-suffering Bulldog thinking: 'Our goalkicking is hopeless. We never nail that crunch goal. It cost us in 2009, and in so many other big games. It's like a disease, handed down through the generations. Breathed in from the Whitten Oval mud. I wouldn't be surprised if they eventually discover it's some sort of bacterial infestation, unleashed when they knocked down the John Gent stand.'

Reasonable, rational, smug, premiership-glutted Hawthorn supporter thinking: 'Oh, for heaven's sake, you Bulldogs supporters do love a melodrama. Settle down and take a breath. Goalkicking is fixable. Just a skill to be worked on and improved. Why on earth should the points kicked in the 2009 preliminary final have anything to do with Jordan Roughead missing an absolute sitter at a critical moment now, right when we really, really, really needed him?' (Sorry, I may be getting my personas mixed up ...)

Flawed, long-suffering Bulldog thinking: 'I just don't like losing very much.'

Reasonable, rational, smug, premiership-glutted Hawthorn supporter thinking: 'Winning's much more fun. And I should know. But you're going to find that out a hell of a lot more over the next few years.'

OUR GOLDEN BOY

We're playing That Certain Club From South Australia. Daily Bailey (his name still eludes me) has just kicked a point. We've been clinging to an eight-point lead for what seems like forever. We've been in front for all but the first few minutes of the match. We've smashed them in clearances, in possessions, in forward entries. Appropriately enough, like dog years, minutes stretch into hours whenever our team is in a suffocatingly close last quarter.

The Crows kick out. But instead of going for the relative safety of the boundary line, one of their backmen launches a massive, bold kick straight down the centre. Spectators and players alike seem caught by surprise, our eyes elsewhere, absorbed in watching the usual efforts to close up space.

But surprise isn't quite the right word to describe the split-second in which it dawns on us, simultaneously, that one man has escaped out the back and is lurking, ready to snaffle the ball, with all our defenders stranded up the ground. That unattended man is Eddie Betts, just as he was too many times in the 2015 elimination final. As he pounces and the inevitable goal comes, our fans let out an excruciating groan. It's a groan that comes with the realisation that, although we've been by far the better team all night, a match is about to slip through our increasingly sweaty palms.

Somebody says: 'Not again, Dogs. Not again.' It may have been me.

The ball's going forward again – into our forward line this time, mercifully. The men in red, white and blue look fierce and determined. Daily Bailey somehow has it again, and guides a perfect, clever kick to the centre half-forward spot. The man who marks it, 50 metres out, is none other than The Bont.

In last year's elimination final, against this same team, with their knack for killing off Bulldog daydreams, The Bont missed two gettable goals. In a match far too much like tonight's, we'd squandered our dominance while our steadier, more experienced opponents nabbed all their chances. Straightaway we fans began to project our anxieties onto The Bont. Footy forums everywhere started anguished debates about whether he and his other precocious teammates were also destined to fall short, unable to reserve their greatest moments for when the Dogs needed them the most.

For me at least, this raises another tormenting question: is it the very fact that we worry like this which makes the weight of our restless hopes and desperation for success too heavy to bear? Is that the reason kids like Griffen and Cooney, or Grant and Johnson before them, begin to lose their starry-eyed, the-sky-is-the-limit idealism? Maybe we are the problem, not them.

My head is in my hands: I don't think I can bear to watch as The Bont prepares to take his kick. The Dogs are only three points ahead; if he kicks a point, there's the all-too-real possibility of another Crows sweep down the ground, defensive mistakes from us, a goal either hard-earned or flukey to snatch the game. Memories of the catastrophic last 90 seconds of our match against the Hawks in Round 3 flutter into my mind as I brace myself for the worst.

Yet I do look up, and with relief I see The Bont looking determined, serious, but not overawed. (I don't quite know what I expected – him in the arms of the trainers, being treated for an anxiety attack?) He strikes the ball with everything in his young but strong legs. The roar begins when the ball is in mid-flight. We don't need to be told to 'make some noise'; we laugh, yell, scream. Something more than a regulation kick to win a game has just happened before our disbelieving eyes. This is, at last, our man who handles the big moment. Who maybe even wanted the big moment.

I think of a moment in Socceroos history, when Harry Kewell, who had begun to have his share of doubters, kicked a magical goal. Commentator Simon Hill captured the euphoria of the moment perfectly: 'Australia's golden boy has come up with a golden goal!'

All the success-starved Bulldogs fans, projecting their dreams onto The Bont, have been hoping for a moment just like this. He's our golden boy.

What a strange experience it is to be a fan, I think, not for the first time, as I leave the ground, elated, euphoric and – mysteriously enough for a person whose greatest exertion was mustering enough courage to watch The Bont seal the game – bone-tired. If he hadn't kicked that goal, if we'd lost the match, it would have destroyed forever all the other magical moments of the match. I wouldn't have wanted to watch again some clas-sic Lair moments, or even his marvellously intuitive tap to an equally smart thinker in Celeb Daniel. There would have been no revelling in four quarters of Men of Mayhem footy, no excited chatter at how Bevo Our Saviour managed to rejig the flat and listless team which had lost to North.

I would have tried to ruthlessly wipe from my memory bank all the efforts of our gallant and undermanned defence, and refused to get misty-eyed over the splendid sight of an All-Australian intercept marker and quality ball-user in top form. (I'm referring of course to 'Keith' Boyd.) The clearance work of Libba, the immensity of effort from Mitch Wallis, the heartening sight of Big Jack Redpath prowling around our forward line and giving Jake some respite, the footy smarts of the only player on the ground who makes Dailey Bailey look like a hulking brute, Toby McLean – all these memories would have been like ashes in our mouths if we'd lost the game.

People less versed in footy psychology might find this puzzling. These are moments worth cherishing and celebrating on their own, they might say. Yet we all know they're not.

Even the immensity of The Bont's game up to that critical moment – the brilliance of his one-handed taps, his clearances and tackles – would have been overshadowed if, instead of a goal, he'd wobbled a miserable point or (a heretical thought!) failed to make the distance. It's unlikely a miss would have been seen in its correct context: as a tired shank from a still very young player who'd given his all. With our history, it would have seemed like yet another message from the universe, another stab of pain in the nerve centre of our collective memories.

The Bont *could* have missed. And yet he didn't.

Watching the game that night is one of our greatest players, Chris Grant. He is shown on the big screen a couple of times, and he looks relaxed. Chris is now a face in the crowd, a husband and father, watching as the new generation take charge of his team. Bruce McAvaney once made a cruel gibe about Chris, one that even he now regrets. He said Grant fell short of the greatness accorded to one of his contemporaries, Wayne Carey, because he'd a history of being unable to kick one of those clutch goals under the most white-hot pressure. I still feel indignant thinking about the insult. Yet I'm so glad, too: that The Bont didn't miss.

As our song is belted out, the coaching staff walk down the aisles. Bob Murphy walks – it's more of a limp – behind them. We applaud him, but Bob doesn't have the roguish twinkle in his eye, the 'wasn't that fabulous' expression that I hoped he might. Like a helpless fan – like us – he'd watched those wrenching, exhilarating, crazy last moments, unable to take a saving mark, to direct a teammate to cover Eddie Betts, to play his role. Nor was he part of the exuberant huddle, the band of brothers who swamped The Bont at that pivotal moment, when The Bont did not miss.

After we'd thrashed the previously undefeated Adelaide early in the 2015 season, the conviction that this team was going to deliver something special took hold in my mind. I've somehow never forgotten my sister saying, out of the blue, as we floated out after the match: 'They're going to do it, this group. They're going to win us a flag one day.'

I've reached for those words like a mantra when there have been moments of doubt. They're drumming around in my brain now, as the joyful crowd disperses, delighted that Our Boys had the steel to at last win a close one: 'They're going to do it. This is the group.'

REIGNING CATS, TIRED DOGS

Hope and fear: they swirl around in equal proportions as we approach our top-of-the-ladder clash against the Cats.

Hope: because that's what Bevo Our Saviour and his troops have instilled, along with confidence, belief and pride. We have faith in the incredible resilience our team have shown to win nine matches, to keep a tenacious grip on a top four spot and withstand an appalling run with injury.

Fear: because we're playing … Geelong.

I can't erase a mental image of the Geelong players, the ultimate professionals, assembling at their home ground. They slap each other on the back, glints in their eyes, ready to cruise in formation down the Princes Highway. They leap in unison onto their gleaming Harley-Davidsons, engines thrumming powerfully, confident of their ability to banish their Bulldog opponents into obscurity and stomp out any premiership pretensions. I'm not fooled by the baby faces of the two leaders out in front of the squad, sporting mirrored sunglasses and blue-and-white-striped bandanas. Beneath the choirboy appearances of Patrick Danger-field and Joel Selwood, as they lead their destructive forces towards Docklands, are a pair of seriously mean badasses.

Just what is it about Geelong? It feels like they're always there, ready to beat up on us in finals. A check of the history books shows that's because ... well, they are always there, ready to beat up on us in finals.

The Dogs haven't exactly been regulars at the pointy end of the season over our 90-odd years in the competition. So surely it's a statistical anomaly that we've encountered the Cats 10 times in the 45 finals we've played in that time? Only twice in those 10 matches, all played at the MCG, have we emerged victorious.

Overall, in our time in the VFL/AFL, we've played Geelong 155 times and won only 56. And our recent performances haven't exactly addressed this imbalance. The last time we beat Geelong was in 2009.

But all this is the past – or it would be, if I didn't keep bringing it up. I try to change the dreary soundtrack of my internal monologue. I remind myself that Bevo Our Saviour undoubtedly has strategies in place to counter the Curse of the Cats. Sure, he's said he has no plans to tag Dangerfield and Selwood. What a card that Bevo is. He's just foxing, right?

I rummage for a few more points on the 'hope' side of the ledger. Perhaps the Cats are flattered by their position on the top of the ladder. They've lost this year to lowly teams such as Carlton and Collingwood. Maybe they've reverted to the quirky flakiness that used to be their lot. (Before those three recent premierships, that is.)

As for Dangerfield and Selwood – well, we've got a more than handy midfield too. Maybe Cats fans are sitting anxiously on the train journey to Melbourne, wringing their hands and saying to each other in slightly hysterical tones, 'Let's hope Chris Scott has got a plan to counter Bontempelli and Stringer. Surely we've got a plan for them?'

Almost from the moment the teams run out onto the ground, my hopeful sentiments are exposed as empty bravado. Is it just an optical illusion created by the hoops on those Geelong jumpers, or are all their players a good 10 centimetres taller and 20 kilos heavier than our lot? Shouldn't WorkCover intervene, to prevent the fresh-faced 18-year-old Bailey Williams from playing in the same half of the ground as that massive monster Tom Hawkins, who weighs in at 108 kilograms?

And I'd thought (or deluded myself into believing) that all their premiership heroes had retired or gone to play with Essendon, but there, limbering up with the confidence of men who probably have pictures of Bulldogs jumpers on their lockers as motivation, are some sickeningly familiar foes: Enright, Mackie, Bartel, Hawkins, Lonergan, Selwood, Taylor.

In line with my apocalyptic vision, the Cats open proceedings with ominous ease. Within minutes Corey Enright looks as though the number 44 on his back stands for the number of possessions he always accumulates against us. He and Mackie, just like in the good old days, flick the ball around flatfooted and curiously tired-looking Bulldogs opponents. Their precise kicks slice across the ground. Our forward pressure is zilch; the Cats are never in trouble at the kick-outs, and outnumber us everywhere.

When the scoreboard shows, before half time, that Geelong have had 15 marks inside their 50-metre zone to our one, nobody is surprised. But we do sink into a familiar depression.

A little rally in the third quarter fizzles out, and soon we are on our way to a hiding, the sort of thrashing that we'd escaped in our three honourable losses so far this season. We look slow, flat, listless. Our trademark desperation has gone, as has our tackling intensity. There's no zing, flair or pizzazz; if the Geelong players aren't breathing down our necks, we fear they are, and make panicky errors. Whenever we try to break the shackles our efforts don't seem daring and exhilarating, just puzzling and inept.

Our mood is glum as we depart the ground. We've been here before, too many times, with the Cats exposing us, even embarrassing us, as pretenders to their throne. As a distraction, I move into pointless indignation. Really, I fume, haven't the Cats had enough premiership glory? After all, the Dogs and Cats were both dashing young teams in 2006, both poised for greatness when emerging stars such as Ryan Griffen and Gary Ablett Junior galloped along the wings in enthralling battles. Yet they went on to win three flags, while we didn't even make a grand final. It seems a bit, well, greedy, for them to be having a resurgence so soon. Wouldn't it be just our luck if our bogey team hit their straps as a top side again just when we're trying to claw our way towards a new story, a different future?

Soon I am clutching at straws. Wasn't it unsporting for the Cats to have continually kicked to whichever of their teammates was being manned by Celeb Daniel? I mean, honestly, if the Geelong players are going to stoop to winning games that way, I don't respect them at all. What kind of example are they setting for the youth of today? They're hypocrites, really, claiming in their song to 'play the game as it should be played'.

After all this huffing and puffing, becoming philosophical takes a while. At least as long as it takes to reach the car park.

But a sense of proportion eventually comes, the knowledge that this result was hardly unexpected, given the age profiles of the two teams. Even by our youthful standards, the team that took on the Cats was inexperienced, with an average of 70 games per player, and with 11 who have played under 50 games. This is normally the profile of a bottom-four club, one which is routinely smashed. In contrast, the Geelong Meanies have an average of 120 games per player. They still have that core of triple premiership stars, and the addition of a fairly handy player called Patrick Dangerfield. Not to mention a lot of players much taller than Celeb Daniel.

In retrospect, it's much more reasonable to view Saturday night as a tipping point in our ability to withstand a growing and frustrating injury toll. The bye has come at the right time for our sore young team.

I find myself delving into the history books, curious to find out when those two finals wins against Geelong occurred. They were, I learn, in the 1950s. Perhaps – you never know – we were Geelong's bogey team back then. After all, we defeated them in the semi-final in 1954 for a place in the grand final, and that win set us up for that one and only (and far too long ago) flag.

Maybe the day the Dogs repeat the deeds of the men of '54 and finally beat those annoyingly good Cats – on the MCG, and in a cut-throat final – will be a circuit-breaker, a sign at last of a new beginning. I begin to visualise how satisfying it will be, this smashing of that spell induced for far too long by those blue-and-white hoops. Perhaps it will come with a burst of Jake the Lair's theatrics, I think. It's the onset of winter, and it's getting harder to hope, and dream, no matter what.

WE'VE GOT
THE CLOSE ONES

It's a little over a year since that thrilling win against Sydney, which Bob Murphy described as 'the best, ever'. The Dogs' victory had announced to a surprised footy world – and to an equally stunned Bulldogs faithful – that they'd well and truly arrived. (Well, actually, we then lost the next three games in a row, but I'd prefer it if inconvenient facts like that didn't intrude on this narrative.)

In the constantly changing footy landscape, many things are different as we go into the 2016 version of our encounter with the Swans. In 2015 the Dogs' resurgence from a disastrous off-season was a feel-good story, and, as with any fairytale, it was enough just to be under its spell. Each win was a novelty to be celebrated for its own sake; with no expectations we enjoyed our spectacular rise, revelled in our devil-may-care style of play, and basked in the new-found freedom that our players so enthusiastically embraced under new coach Bevo (who was not yet 'Our Saviour' ... but we had our suspicions). In 2016, while we're not favourites against the top-of-the-ladder Swans, much more is expected – indeed, much more should be expected. Brave, gallant showings will not suffice. Not for where we want to go.

Yet over the bye weekend, as the piercing cold of a Melbourne winter descended, our disappointing showing against Geelong loomed large in our memories. It cast a shadow over our achievements in getting to nine wins and four losses despite an appalling run of injuries. And as we dropped to a more vulnerable position in the bottom reaches of the eight, a little wave of apprehension rippled through us.

The ever-fickle commentators are scrambling to downgrade our premiership hopes: the chatter becomes a din. They've decided that we're still too young to make a real impact in September, and that our injury toll has unsettled us too much. These critics remind us that we have not yet beaten a top four side. They point to a lack of scoring power, especially in our losses, as a worrying sign.

In fact, on the morning of our match against the Swans, I hear the 'experts' discussing the eight and who might be vulnerable to dropping out for Port Adelaide by season's end. The Bulldogs will be that team, they agree, despite the fact that we've recently disposed of the Power, and on their home turf. I'm unsure whether to seethe at the unjustified lack of respect continually accorded to our club or listen for a moment to the whispering ghosts of seasons past, which say they may just be right.

Bevo Our Saviour is attuned to a different vibe, and a different radio frequency. For our match against the Swans, he has rattled the cage, bringing in five new players. The most exciting and emotional news is the return of Clay Smith, more than 13 months after his third knee reconstruction.

My thoughts return to the thrilling 2015 win. How, I wonder, could moments like Easton Wood's Superman-style goal, and his incredible one-handed pickup of a greasy ball to save us the game with seconds to go, ever be surpassed by anything that might transpire today? Last year's win was so perfect, so wonderful, that it still shines like a diamond in my memory.

Yet in the wake of Bob's injury there is now a tinge of melancholy in that recollection. It is bittersweet now to remember how we shared his overflowing emotions post-match, his elation as he realised his premiership dream wasn't over, his joy at riding the magic carpet with his precocious young teammates. And though the match took place hundreds of kilometres away, somehow that day we couldn't have been any closer, more as one with our captain and our team.

The Libba Sisters convene, taking up our positions on the couch in the Rising Sun apartments again; we ensure we sit in exactly the same spots as during last year's win. (Sure, you can call it a silly superstition. But there is no way I'm prepared to risk a situation in which a perplexed Luke Beveridge, facing the media post-match, looks down his list of statistics as he tries to explain what went wrong and realises, with consternation, that the all-important 'Libba Sisters on the Couch' metric has cost Our Boys the game.)

The Dogs look sprightly and switched-on in the first quarter, compared to their lacklustre showing against the Cats. Frustratingly, though, our 13 inside-50 entries yield just one goal and one point.

The Libbas, of course, spot countless missed frees to the Dogs, openly disparage the commentary team, and shield our eyes in terror whenever Clay Smith goes near the ball. Hearteningly, this is often. I think about a story that has gone around: that on that awful day in 2015 when his knee buckled, Clay returned to the field because he believed – and for a moment accepted – that he would never play again.

It's impossible not to hold our breath whenever Clay is in a pack. Fear for his wellbeing, though, is soon replaced by a renewed appreciation of his play: Clay is unswerving in his fanatical commitment, desperate and uncompromising. And as he lays crunching tackles and flings himself into every contest, we remember that this is not just a feel-good story of a comeback; this marks the return of a vital player, whose contribution and toughness are going to be of immense value to our team as the season goes on.

The first quarter is something of a standoff, but the second quarter opens with the mercurial Jake the Lair slamming through two trademark goals. Single-handedly he threatens to bust the game open in the same way that he bullocks through the Swans' defence. But his contribution too quickly fades away. Meanwhile, at the other end of the ground Buddy Franklin exudes danger and menace. (The Libbas still think he's carrying a couple too many kilos ...) He dwarfs even the powerfully built Marcus Adams, who in the presence of this superstar looks every bit the inexperienced and nervous 11-gamer that he is.

The half-time break is an opportunity for contemplation. Hundreds of kilometres from the match, it's easy enough to be critical. Several players are not at their best. The Libbas agree: Our Boys look a little flat.

We're unprepared for a third-quarter explosion. The Dogs crank up their attack on the ball to fearless, insane levels. Suddenly there are Dogs players rampaging everywhere; there's run, there's space opening up. We stun the opposition and wreak havoc on the SCG.

Leading the charge is Tom Liberatore. Three goals are either directly his or created by him. Some players float through games with all the time in the world, relying on languid ability and freakish talent; others, like our Libba the Second, will themselves into contests through sheer intensity. He wrests balls out of hands, he dominates every contest, he tackles with the demented ferocity of his famous dad.

Not to be outdone, Marcus Bontempelli enters the stage. Some of the things The Bont does in this third quarter, when he amasses 13 possessions, are downright ridiculous. There is an almost hypnotic passage of play in which he scoops up the ball from the turf in the Swans' forward line, runs at full tilt, bounces the ball, handballs it to another player, who returns it to him, and then, as a Swans player closes in on him, perfectly handballs backwards over his head to a running teammate. He somehow keeps running and presents himself in the forward line. It is rather like those imaginary games little boys (and girls now too) play in their heads: 'Bonti to Bonti to Bonti, and who does he kick it to? Bonti!' The fact that he doesn't take the mark (though he very nearly does) is the only thing that shows you Our Golden Boy is occasionally – just occasionally, mind – a human.

There's tension aplenty at three-quarter time. Deep breaths, calm and nerves of steel are required, and not just from the rather agitated Libbas. We watch Our Boys gather around Bevo. Each week all teams and all players, no matter what the situation of the game, however far behind they might be, and even whether the result matters or not, form this ritualistic huddle and emit snarls of intent before the last quarter. It used to amuse me when we did this even in the most putrid of matches and horrid of seasons. I'm intrigued to know what gets said. Perhaps I'd be disappointed if I did.

The Bulldogs' faces are something else as they listen to Bevo. I see Celeb Daniel, his eyes locked onto his coach; our pocket-sized dynamo is almost in the armpits of The Bont, who's under the same spell. I marvel at our game, how these two different young men with their different skills – one the power athlete, the other the pure footballer – can both play this game at the highest level.

Whatever mysterious whispers Bevo transmits to his troops, one thing is certain: the Swans will come back at us. We are – amazingly, given our injury catastrophes – the number-one defensive team in the competition, but Sydney lurk at number two. We are the third-best team for contested possessions, yet they are ahead of us at number one. They've still got the aura, the knowhow, the experience of a recent premiership team and regular finalist. And they have the X factor: the competition's best player, Buddy Franklin, who is about to cut loose.

Franklin destroys us in minutes. He's too big, too powerful, too strong. Too overwhelmingly talented. The Swans take the lead. There are still 11 minutes to go. Our season, our top four hopes, our credentials as a club capable of beating the top teams, especially after our capitulations to North and Geelong – all are now on the line.

The Swans pound into their forward line. We're reeling, like a bloodied boxer on the ropes. Just one more goal will surely sink us. Standing firm time and again are Dale Morris, Matthew Boyd and Easton Wood. Their desperation holds the Swans out, but there must be a point at which even their heroic efforts won't be enough. And even if they do keep holding out, there's a question: how are we to manufacture that elusive answering goal?

The Libbas have abandoned, again, their lucky spots on the couch. Once again there's uproar in the Rising Sun apartments. Our Boys have been so brave. But the minutes are relentlessly ticking by.

By sheer will, we begin to turn the tide. Now it's the Dogs who are attacking, but with the advantage of the lead, the Swans turn our forward line into a sea of congestion, crowded with players from both sides. There is not a chink of room. The Swans try to clear the ball out, but Jackson Macrae sends it back in. Clay Smith applies a monster tackle, and Wally hands off the ball to Celeb. In the frenzied atmosphere, this 19-year-old has the stillness, poise and calmness to make the perfect decision and somehow execute a perfect kick to his teammate.

It's The Bont. Of course, it had to be The Bont. He's kicked crucial goals to win us two close games this year, helping to rewrite our history of failure on big occasions. The ball couldn't be in safer hands ... could it?

There's hardly time to ponder the question: The Bont makes his own perfect pass, to Jason Johannisen. JJ is still 50 metres out, though at a better angle. The shot at goal, with less than 30 seconds to go, with so much at stake, is far from easy.

I'm not sure if he's the man for a moment like this, to win us the game while 33,000 Sydney fans are screaming their lungs out. He's missed nine weeks through a badly torn hamstring; this is his first game back. His body and fitness have been tested in this ferocious, titanic struggle.

I can't believe how self-assured JJ looks. (Much more so than the hyperventilating Libba Sisters, who lock our arms around each other as we wait.) He is another former rookie in our team. I can't remember any massive anticipation around his first game, as I can with The Bont's or The Lair's. I can't remember a moment where we began to see him as an indispensable player, an elite talent. But as he steers through the goal, as though it's just a regulation shot at training at the Whitten Oval, I think – I know – that moment has well and truly arrived.

There's two seconds to go. I regret to report that this is long enough for me to imagine a nightmare scenario in which we stupidly allow five men in the centre square, the Swans are awarded a free kick, and then a 50-metre penalty is awarded against Will Minson for arguing about it. (I guess this 'hope' and 'positivity' business is still a work in progress.) But as soon as the ball is bounced, the siren sounds. Our magical, maddening, wonderful team have delivered us another jewel for the memory bank. It hasn't surpassed that 2015 moment when Easton saved the game, but it will sit beside it, as the day that JJ kicked his match-winning goal. And maybe the most telling thing of all was that JJ demanded the ball from The Bont. Unlike some of the more fragile teams of days gone by, he actually *wanted* to take the kick, and backed his own talent, not content to be secretly relieved that the responsibility lay with someone else.

The Dogs celebrate and run around the SCG. It's not rainy and sodden like last year, but we are victors again. Libba the Second, whose dynamic third quarter swayed the game, shares an embrace with his Brownlow medallist dad, who'll probably be very happy to be known one day simply as Tom Liberatore's father. The players run down the race. Bob – a spectator today, as he will be all season – greets them with the widest of smiles.

The boys belt out the song with extra fervour. Another test passed. Another step taken.

When the song ends, Easton, Matthew Boyd and The Bont find each other for an enormous hug. These three leaders have had to fill the void left by Bob. It's not a void, though, really, because the team out there still has Bob's heart – as well as young men such as JJ, Celeb, Libba and Wally, who are mastering new ways to win those close ones, learning the steel and the belief that we'll need in September. They're watched over by those old stagers Boyd and Morris, who have the glint in their eyes of men saying: 'There's a flag coming soon and I've got to be a part of it.'

A few hours later, it's still hard to come down from the high of an extraordinary win. I find myself remembering again the brilliant third quarter played by The Bont, our once-in-a-lifetime player who is such a joy to watch.

A few weeks ago The Bont became the AFL's youngest-ever winning captain, leading us to victory in a must-win game against the Eagles. Just 20 years old, he'd gathered the boys around him for a pep talk in the moments before the match. The Bont must have done okay, because I saw Matthew Keith Boyd – almost 15 years his senior, and a former skipper himself – give him an affectionate ruffle of the hair and pat on the back. A passing of the baton, I guess. 'The kid's all right,' I imagine the gruff Boyd saying as he ran off to take up his backline position, a reborn defender playing his own part in creating a future that's so near.

THE BIG STEAL

It's three-quarter time at Docklands. Yet even though we're only one goal down, I've got serious doubts about whether the lethargic Dogs have the run or the will to get over a tenacious Richmond outfit. The Tigers, whose fans have endured almost as much as ours over the past three decades, this week took a pounding in the media. They've turned up more desperate, fiercer and more committed to the contest.

There's frustration in the muttered conversations of Bulldogs fans as we dissect what's gone wrong – how, with a top four spot as the prize, we could possibly be playing so badly. We can't fathom why our players time and again are choosing poor options, handballing to flatfooted teammates, missing tackles and generally showing a depressing lack of the run and zest that we've come to expect this season.

I've got an inkling of what the problem is, however: I've forgotten to bring my lucky Bonti badge.

Thirty minutes later the rather stunned Dogs fans are

certainly not echoing E.J.'s famous catchcry – 'I tipped this!' – but are channelling his equally memorable words: 'Oh, what a bloody relief!' Having previously claimed that this was one of the worst games I'd ever watched, I now hasten home, keen to watch the last quarter once, twice or even four times.

At first I'm just thankful that we dodged a bullet. Then I begin to reflect on why and how we pulled it off, when so many players were below their best. After all, I've witnessed this phenomenon in reverse: there have been countless times when, like Richmond on Saturday night, the Dogs have been the underdogs, fighting and scrapping and arguably more deserving of a win, but have still blown the four points. We've known the pain they're now experiencing, of being unable to finish a match off because we're playing a team with more composure, more will, more experience in the clutch moments, more steel. Could this mean, then, that our Dogs are on the verge of becoming one of those teams?

We now have a new-found knack of winning the close ones. Our last four wins have all been tight: we've scraped home by a total of just 25 points. There have been come-from-behind wins, wins where we've withstood the sort of strong challenge that has so often been our undoing, wins where clutch goals under the most intense pressure have been kicked. How on earth has Bevo Our Saviour quarantined our flaky club from its reputation as fragile in the clinches?

Well, the main reason is that, at long last, we have leaders who stand up when we need them. With the loss of Bob our world had tipped on its axis. It wasn't just his leadership, his on-field inspiration, but also the intangible way he seems to get our club and its romantic, quixotic, often downright painful tussle with its unsuccessful history and its struggle to forge a new story.

It felt like a loss that couldn't be overcome. And yet new leaders have stepped into the void, tentatively at first, and then with growing confidence.

Easton Wood initially looked overawed, a little inhibited, in the role. Yet his leadership has been critical in many of our close wins; on Saturday night he was simply breathtaking in the nerve-racking last quarter, especially when he had the courage and dare to launch an electrifying run away from Jack Riewoldt. But you can also see that in this team leadership is a shared responsibility, as players initiate moves, remind each other where to run and, as we saw against Sydney, don't shirk the responsibility of a big moment.

Quiet achievers who play their role week in and week out keep the ship steady. Men such as Liam Picken and Jack Macrae don't get the accolades or adulation that some bigger names do. They're both so low-key that their nicknames seem to be … Picko and Jacko. The only number 42 guernseys around are probably those of Liam's three little children, while those wearing number 11 probably had their jumpers handed down from fans of a former cult hero, gangly ruckman Peter Street.

Jacko came to us as a high draft pick. Even back then he was overshadowed, though, because the name called out straight after his was Jake Stringer's. The skinny kid, who stood with a shy smile next to the formidable Lair, who already had the body of a man, was known as an outside runner. Yet it's rarely noted just how many of his possessions are now contested, how many times his head is over the ball. Not for the first time Jacko led the tackle count on Saturday night. Many of them – crunching ones, too – were laid in the heat of the last-quarter battle.

Picko was a rookie, a late bloomer who could so easily never have played a match. His club, Williamstown, actually paid his first year's salary so that we'd give him a chance. I've seen Liam Picken around the western suburbs. He looks barely 13 years old, and so much slighter than you would imagine. But in a team that's not really known as having a streak of mean, the cherubic Picken is one man in the red, white and blue who opposition players dread encountering at the bottom of a pack.

Equally unheralded are the efforts of what Bob calls 'The Men's Department' – our defence. They seem like a slightly ragtag, unglamorous bunch, yet only Sydney's has been meaner in 2016.

Then there's the fact that three father-sons feature in our best players. Between them, their fathers played 639 games for our club. In Mitch Wallis's fierce attack on the ball and curly blond locks you can see our former captain Steve. Libba the Second has his dad Tony's zeal for a crunching tackle (in a recent match, he came close to breaking the all-time record). And in his love of the niggle and his ability to frustrate the opposition you can definitely see the heritage of the little champ with the enormous heart. Meanwhile, our other father-son selection, Lachie Hunter, who this time last year was on the fringes of selection, has been transformed into our highest possession winner, a hard-running ball magnet. (While I certainly don't want to spark any undue speculation, Lachie – as a prolific ball gatherer, a left-footer and a blond number seven – frequently reminds me of Scott West rather than his father, Mark, a dour defender.)

One of my favourite daydreams is to imagine the moment that Lachie Hunter, Mitch Wallis and Tom Liberatore burst through the banner together in a grand final. And I can't help but feel that these three, when that day comes, will have an extra motivation, as well as the DNA, to make the extra tackle, run the extra step and banish forever the memory of the heartache their famous dads went through.

The final wildcards in our transformation from chokers to winners are, of course, Marcus Bontempelli and Jake Stringer. In all our close wins you can see the hand – the outlandishly big hands – of The Bont. Against the Tigers, our lacklustre performance demanded a match-winner, someone to will us over the line, the big-game performer for whom successive Bulldogs teams have cried out for too many years. And from the moment at the start of the tight fourth quarter when The Bont scooped up the ball one-handed and launched the chain of possessions that would result in our comeback, you knew he would again be that man.

His fellow prodigy, Jake the Lair, has been a tad out of sorts lately. His trademark bullocking bursts have more often resulted in holding the ball than goal of the year. And in the third quarter a feeble missed tackle apparently earned the ire of Bevo Our Saviour. Even I, his most devoted fan, grimaced at that, and silently wished that Jake was sometimes, just sometimes, a bit less of a lair.

But oh, how he made up for it. He kicked two superb long goals that never looked like missing, and then, when those pesky Tigers still kept threatening, The Bont freakishly extracted the ball from a clearance and, with his trademark over-the-head handball, found Jake, who was able to barnstorm into a goal.

As the crowd made an unbelievable roar at the combining of these two extraordinary talents (is there anything better than

Bontempelli and Stringer coming together in one delectable passage?), we see the X factor that all those other Bulldogs teams – gritty, brave, unlucky or (could it be as simple as this?) maybe just not quite good enough – could never draw on in the fiercest of finals contests.

But it still might be a good idea if I remember to pack my lucky Bonti badge.

FOOTY, THE GAME
OF HEARTACHE

Round 1 seems a lifetime ago. Back then, footy, the beautiful game, had us in its magical thrall. And all things were still possible. While thrashing Freo in the brilliant sunshine, Our Boys were tanned, superbly fit, brimming with hope, confidence, desire and self-belief. That day could not have felt further away as we arrive on Saturday night at the stadium to confront a team that has so often given us pain: the Saints. The roof is closed, but even so we're rugged up against the biting cold wind, the bleakness of a grey and drizzly Melbourne winter.

Richmond coach Damien Hardwick once described July as 'big boys' month'. Providing the ultimate test of desire, fitness and self-belief, it's a time when strong minds and even stronger bodies prevail, and the deficiencies of pretenders are ruthlessly exposed. Despite a testing run with injuries the Dogs sit in the top four. And although we're playing one of our bogey teams, Our Boys will, I'm sure, meet yet another challenge and grind out the crucial four points.

As we walk out of the stadium, having lost the match and so much more, it feels like footy's version of the winter solstice has arrived. The darkest day, the point where hope seems to shrivel, where one too many obstacles have been flung in our faces.

At this point we don't know the full extent of Mitch Wallis's leg injury. Just that it's bad – real bad. We're pretty sure that Jack Redpath has done his knee, for the third time. No one can say why Dale Morris, our warrior braveheart in the backline, was unable to take the field for the second half. But even the sight of him in his tracksuit top brings shivers of unease.

My mother has stayed up in Cairns, where she'd watched the Dogs' workmanlike win against Gold Coast last week. She sends a text imbued with Irish fatalism: 'God doesn't like the Bulldogs very much.'

The Dogs lost by 15 points. We didn't score in the last quarter. Literally. We couldn't even scrounge a rushed behind. My feet never thawed out the whole game. There hadn't been enough jumping up and down with excitement; there were few inspirational passages to bring us up off our seats and get the circulation flowing. Not many moments in which the stadium rocked with the Bulldogs chant, and chilblain-infested toes could do the stamp.

There's a heaviness among the fans, mirroring what unfolded on the field. Doubts, never far away when you're a Bulldogs fan, creep in. Our dysfunctional forward line. The calibre of our second-tier players. The fatigue of the players, the missing dare and spark. The skills, or mystifying lack thereof. The wrong options taken time and again. 'Footy,' I think to myself. 'It's a stupid game after all.'

I arrive home and, with sinking heart, begin reading about the injury Wally sustained in the last quarter. He has broken both bones in his leg. I listen to the harrowing description of the scenes in the room from an ABC reporter whose voice trembles as he describes the terrible scene. Mitch's screams of agony were heard by his teammates, friends and family. Shell-shocked players were in tears. Bob Murphy, we hear, broke down, sobbing uncontrollably.

In the rooms with Mitch are men for whom this agony is all too real. Dale Morris and Jake Stringer know what it's like to fracture a leg. I recall a poignant article in which Dale's wife talked about the dreary, awful details that an injury like this entails: of Dale in a wheelchair, needing help to be showered – every second day because it was so difficult – and toileted. Dale, aged over 30 at the time, the premiership window that he'd been part of seemingly slammed shut, wondered if he would ever play again.

Stringer broke his leg in the same almost ridiculous way as Mitch, somehow kicking the back of his own limb. He was 17 years old, and being touted as a number-one draft pick. With the horrible injury he was suddenly hovering on the precipice of the footy scrapheap. Jake has spoken of what it was like to watch elderly neighbours lap him as he limped around the footy oval in those long, tedious months of rehabilitation.

Most of us fans can't know the pain, physical and emotional, that these players endure. The fear they must experience every time they go out there, that this time it could be them, stretchered off to the polite but apprehensive applause of the subdued fans. The man closest to Mitch when the hideous injury happened was the baby of our team, 19-year-old Josh Dunkley. How must he have felt, seeing Mitch with a bone protruding horribly through his skin, knowing that this is the risk he too runs every time he takes part in this thrilling, brutal, dangerous game of ours?

At times like this I sense the players retreating inside their own bubble, a world that only they know – because to them, the club and their teammates are home, workplace, friendship group and family all at once. Only they can truly appreciate Bob's grim humour when he tweeted about donning hospital-issue undies and hairnets before being wheeled into surgery. Only they can relate to the indignities of needing help from a wife or girlfriend (or, worse still, a parent) whenever they need to use the toilet. The loneliness at 3 a.m. when you're racked with pain or, as our former player and current commentator Nathan Brown once described, lying drenched in sweat from the painkillers and the agony that even a sheet over your injured leg can spark. And the doubts about whether you'll come back as good as you once were. Whether you will come back at all.

And now our footy season lies in the balance. In Saturday night's performance, even before the injuries, we saw a team whose resilience had begun to crack, who looked weary of the effort, who've seen one too many teammates go down, who couldn't muster yet again the urgency, the intense approach of a must-win game.

The headiness of Round 1 and the lure of a new season with its tantalising horizon still ahead now seem like a technicolour dream. Everything is monochrome. We're stranded in the bleakest and toughest stretch of a long and arduous season. The goal that kept the players focused as they trained on 40-degree days or climbed the hills of the Great Ocean Road on their bikes – the dream of spring days, finals footy and more – is, right now, so very far away.

For the fans, there is the pragmatic realisation that these new body-blows make our 2016 dream that much harder. We know that not just this week's injuries but also the cumulative effect of the unusually heavy toll this year could be starting to wear us down. Yet even as we try to turn our minds to the question of how we will regroup and who needs to step up, there is a sorrow at what has befallen our injured players that is more than just a calculation of the impact on our premiership hopes.

Quaint as it may seem in an era of fans as 'stakeholders' and ham-fisted gimmicks to enhance our 'match-day experience', the club and the players are so much a part of our lives that we too have our own sense of sadness at what they're enduring. While we're outside the inner sanctum, it's not far-fetched to say that watching the physical and mental pain of those who are injured, and of those who are close to them, brings us our own measure of grief. The players are the carriers of our dream, the living representatives of our beloved club, and so we are connected with them and invested in them – even though we might have never spoken a word to any of them, or had no more contact with them beyond a high-five along the boundary line.

We start to bond with them when they're awkward, spotty draftees, we look forward with over-the-top enthusiasm to their first games, we build stories around them based on a few stilted interviews, we delight in their progress, and we hope (and pray) for them to succeed. Our knowledge of them is sketchy and incomplete, snippets based on how they present on the field and the carefully crafted images that the club puts forward. But some of them, we feel – we are sure – are special from the outset.

Mitch Wallis has occupied a special place in our imaginings, the boy who grew up to wear the colours of his dad's footy club. Steve Wallis was undoubtedly in the rooms on this harrowing night. He once suffered a broken leg too, as a 17-year-old. Steve was appointed our captain at the age of just 24; he played 261 games. The last six of these, in the dismal *Year of the Dogs* season, 1996, he competed with the agony of a broken hand. Mitch has his dad's curly locks. He's a future captain too, many who know him say; he proudly wears the most famous Bulldog jumper of all, the number three of E.J. and Chris Grant.

So we share just a little of the pain of Mitch, and that of fan favourite Big Jack Redpath, and we are both afraid and misty-eyed whenever Clay Smith shows that, after almost three years in total on the sidelines, his appetite for a ferocious tackle has not diminished.

As I've tried to shrug off the 'Danny from Droop Street' pessimism, which was built on too many years of underachievement and disappointment, so too have I tried to rid myself of the feeling, so common among Dogs fans, that our club is cursed. It's hard not to lapse back into that mindset as we ask why we could be so unlucky again – why, when the future is as bright as we've ever imagined, so many have been struck down. You could hear it in the voices of so many on Saturday night as we grappled with this new challenge, when we've already had to weather so many. My mum indeed captured the mood: *God doesn't like the Bulldogs very much.*

Of course we will all begin to claw back optimism. As dogs do, we will retreat to lick our wounds, before slowly, painfully moving on. We'll start to talk about who'll come in for the injured players, how we can regain our mojo, how much of the season there still is to play. The holy grail is still there to be won.

Next week we play the Cats. At the Cattery. They are invincible there at the best of times. Not the best opportunity for us to rejuvenate our season. But Jake will be back, and maybe even Dahl. Bevo Our Saviour's bound to have a few tricks up his sleeve. We've won 12, lost five – still a great season by anyone's standards. We're not done yet, we say defiantly.

Photos begin appearing on Instagram: Wally from his hospital bed, looking pale, but giving a thumbs-up. The image makes me go searching for that article about Dale Morris. I need to read again about how, after almost 18 months on the sidelines, he made his way back to take his place at his club, alongside his teammates and the fans.

Dale described those awful few hours after he broke his leg, moments that Mitch will be living his own version of now too. 'I'd had the X-rays and I was lying there with a million things going through my head and in walked Matty Boyd. He'd come straight from the game. I don't even think he'd had a shower, and he just sat with me. We had a little bit of a chat, but he didn't even have to say anything.' Another teammate, the injury-plagued Tom Williams, had brought Dale a laptop loaded with dozens of movies – 'he knew what was ahead of me' – and Daniel Cross's wife, Sam, dropped off some containers of homemade pasta sauce at the Morris home.

Although Morris faced months on the sidelines, that weekend confirmed what he had always known: that Whitten Oval was and would always remain his second home. 'If anything, it really felt like I was even more a part of a team,' he said. 'That's the beauty of the Bulldogs.'

'Footy,' I think. 'The game of heartache.'

WE CAN BE HEROES

One day a few years ago, as I was leaving a Bulldogs match, I came across a man pushing a twin pram. Fast asleep inside were two babies, only a few weeks old. They were wearing little Bulldogs jumpers, and their pram was decorated with red, white and blue ribbons.

This was deep in the interminable gloom of the 2011–14 era. Ten-goal drubbings, a grimly defensive style of footy and a dearth of star power: that was our lot. We were excruciatingly bad, at one point losing nine games on the trot.

I caught the eye of the twins' dad as he trundled along with an all-too-familiar air of stoicism. 'Teaching them resilience,' he explained with a wry smile.

Resilience. It's a term bandied about a lot in the lead-up to our match against Geelong. The players are dealing with the horrific leg injury to their teammate Mitch Wallis, not to mention a third knee reconstruction for Jack Redpath, with 'resilience', Bevo Our Saviour tells the media scrum. Endearingly, he could not hide his own tears and quavering voice as he spoke. Another reason to love our Plantagenet-lookalike, Willy-Wonka-quoting, skateboard-riding coach.

But when the team selections for our clash with Geelong are announced on the Thursday night I wonder if even Bevo is conceding the match as a certain defeat. The losses of Wally, Redpath and Dale Morris were expected. But we had no inkling that our defence would be further hit by the loss of the two Matthews, Boyd and Suckling, who are both out with Achilles strains. The team that is named will run out as the youngest and least experienced of all those fielded on the weekend. With an average of 23 years and 10 months and just 66 games, we've eclipsed teams such as Melbourne, Carlton and Essendon, whose regular thrashings were being explained away as inevitable given their age profiles.

And we are facing the Cats on a cold, wet night at their home – a fortress from which, as I imagine perennial voice-over man Craig Willis pretentiously intoning, few Bulldogs teams have ever emerged victorious. In fact, even the legendary E.J. Whitten, so the story goes, never once drove back down that highway a winner.

The Geelong dynasty which began in 2007 is still very much alive, with at least six (it is too depressing to do an exact count) of those triple premiership players in the line-up. And tonight those annoyingly good Cats will be even more fired up – as if the sight of our red, white and blue jumpers isn't sufficient. They are celebrating milestones in the glorious careers of two of those fabled premiership heroes – and serial Bulldogs tormentors – Corey Enright and Jimmy Bartel. Their crowd will be revved up, parochial and at fever pitch. Only a small contingent of Dogs fans will be there. For once I'm not one of them. It's my own small protest at the exorbitant price the Geelong club demands for the small number of available seats.

The Cats cantered away from us a few weeks ago by ten goals, when our list was in much better health. As I settle on the couch I can't see any way our depleted team can avoid a shellacking.

But our players, right from the opening bounce, have different ideas. They stun us with their intensity, their overwhelming determination to win. You'd think that last week's horrible events might have made them hesitant; that seeing a teammate screaming in agony might lead to moments of tentativeness, might sharpen their instinct for self-preservation. Yet they are fiercer, braver, more committed than ever before. The footy world would have excused, even accepted a heavy loss. But Our Boys are demonstrating the most difficult form of courage. It's the courage to believe.

Leading the way with an imperious performance is Libba the Second. He is playing, you feel, for the wounded Mitch Wallis, his fellow father-son recruit and lifelong mate, as much as himself. Despite his own injury woes – last year's knee reconstruction, as well as a visit to hospital with broken ribs only a couple of weeks ago – Libba plays as though his own oversized will can drag us over the line.

It is a little more surprising to see another Tom being instrumental in our impressive start: everyone's favourite whipping boy, the Bulldogs' answer to Jack Watts, he of the constantly discussed pay cheque, Tom Boyd. There's always been a rather placid air about big Tom, little sense that he can hurl his big frame around in the wrecking-ball style of Clay Smith, and little evidence so far that inside him burns the flame of a fierce competitive athlete. But he's apparently had enough of the gibes, the recent suggestions that, having struggled with both form and fitness, he should nobly offer to give up his huge salary. Under pressure that's unimaginable for a 20-year-old, on this Friday night he shows the 'blue chip' talent that Bevo has talked about, the champion he can become.

The first-quarter siren sounds with the Dogs only one point down. The Cats look, if not shell-shocked, at least nettled and aggrieved. Our depleted team have reached somewhere deep, somewhere perhaps even they didn't know they could, and shaken a defiant fist in the direction of the footy universe. They are playing with a heightened recklessness, perhaps on behalf of – or because of – their injured comrades. And I so wish that I could be there, to stand together with my fellow Bulldogs fans and applaud them.

The second quarter begins, and like soldiers we slowly concede ground in a war of attrition. The Cats start to realise that there is no need to join our players and scrabble at the bottom of the pack. They can afford to have a player standing outside, ready to coolly sweep the ball downfield, where our defensive gaps are painfully exposed. The toll of our relentless efforts, our frenzied domination with so little effect on the scoreboard, threatens to – but never quite does – grind us down. The days of dazzling Round 1's 'sexy' footy are long gone. It's hand-to-hand combat in which we now must engage.

And now we see, with disbelief, that our hardiest soldier, Libba, is off the ground. Yet again the wretched sight of an essential player squirming in pain, concerned doctors by his side. Libba will not return for the rest of the match. The news begins to filter through. His injury is a bad one. It's the same as the one that kept Carlton's Marc Murphy out for an entire season

Another of our best, Luke Dahlhaus, who's lit us up with his trademark energy and enthusiasm in his first match back after missing two months because of injury, begins to tire. Umpiring decisions don't go our way. The Geelong players start to exude that air they've always had over us; they look taller, stronger, fresher, faster. More … uninjured.

Yet even though the Cats' authority over the match grows, it's never unchallenged. A few times it looks like a dam wall is about to break and they will rampage over the top of us, but we bob up irrepressibly again – I'll never quite know how. We're still threatening, still surging, even in the last quarter, when we lose yet another player, Jackson Macrae, to what looks like a badly torn hamstring. Our low-key, tireless runner, unappreciated outside the Bulldogs' own fans, had been doing a fine job on Joel Selwood, and still accumulated plenty of the ball himself in the first three quarters.

Old-fashioned words come to my mind as the final siren sounds, and the Dogs register a 25-point loss: gallantry, grace. We'd played the game, as a certain song that we've heard too many times goes, 'as it should be played'. Our Boys stay on the ground as Enright and Bartel are chaired off. Their heads are held high. They aren't losers. They've just lost a game. We've had 10-goal wins that haven't left me feeling as proud as this.

In some of the Bulldogs' more painful seasons, throughout tedious, repetitive losses, often I concentrated on unearthing one little gem of hope, one little moment to be proud of. Sometimes it was a first-gamer in whom we could invest our hopes and fantasies, or a plodding journeyman who had somehow, unexpectedly, had a breakthrough game. It could be, and often was, a moment of Daniel Cross madness as he backed fearlessly into a pack.

There were many nuggets to choose from on Friday. But there are two that I know I will always cherish. The first was the vision of Libba on the boundary line, heavily strapped. Libba would have known that with the finals tantalisingly close, he faced weeks out injured, as well as the surgeon's knife. He prowled the sideline, watching the game as intently as the most devoted fan, clapping his teammates, urging them on.

The other nugget was the splendid sight of The Bont taking the opportunity to set Joel Selwood smartly back down on his backside when the Geelong skipper was getting mouthy. Like all Bulldogs fans for so many years, The Bont looked sick and tired of being pushed around by Geelong. Ah, The Bont. Exquisite skills – check. The leadership and character of a champion – check. Just the right amount of aggression, just the right time to make a statement – wouldn't you know it, our Golden Boy has the right stuff for that as well.

And yet, while we're proud, we fans, who have been patient so long, must absorb the knowledge that we have to be patient once again. We'd nurtured hopes that in this even season, with no standout team, we could somehow snatch an unexpected flag (though, after a 61-year drought, the words 'snatch' and 'unexpected' aren't exactly what I'm reaching for). It's getting harder to imagine us, with our unprecedented injury toll, slogging our way through gruelling finals and featuring on grand final day. But, judging by Friday night, Our Boys aren't accepting that as an inevitability. Not one little bit.

Those little twins in their Bulldog jumpers must be pre-schoolers by now. Maybe, like my own little boy at that age, they insist on starting each day by running through a banner – a sheet I was required to hang from a doorway for this purpose. I imagine them running around the backyard, kicking a footy with their patient dad. They probably have the numbers four and nine on their backs, like most western-suburbs kids I see wearing red, white and blue. Or they might be wearing 21, for Libba. Number three, for Wally. They're learning resilience. Bulldog resilience.

THE SUM OF US

Just when did the Kangaroos morph into the most irritating team in the competition? I'm excluding, of course, the Acronyms – GWS – because they're not a real club. And the Crows, for obvious reasons; 'least likeable' seems far too mild for the hideous memories that team conjures up. Then there's the superiority of the Bourgeois Blues. As for the 'whatever it takes' arrogance of Essendon ... All right, I admit there are a lot of teams I don't like. North are right up there. That's all I'm saying.

Our two clubs should perhaps share some affinity, some sort of kindred spirit. Culturally, there are similarities: both are smaller, working-class clubs, which often struggle to make themselves heard among the clamour and din of bigger and more successful teams. (With four flags, North is actually well ahead of us ... but then pretty much everyone is.) The two clubs are geographically close as well – though that's never brought about a sense of camaraderie with a certain neighbour of ours, which hails from the posh side of the west's scenic attraction, the Maribyrnong.

I've never had any truck with ludicrous concepts such as having a 'second team', or (why?) a 'soft spot' for an opposition club. However, given that North are not one of the teams against which we have a particularly abysmal win–loss ratio (these things are always relative, of course), I feel I should have, if not affection, then at least less animosity towards them than I do.

I suspect (in fact I'm sure) it's the Scott brothers factor. Honestly, is there any free kick to the opposition that Brad Scott ever considers justified? His incredulous reaction to any infringement awarded against his team brings to mind a headline in an Australian newspaper when the England cricket team was losing, none too graciously: 'Can the Poms be beaten fairly?'

I've never been a fan of North's squadron of fake tough guys, who seem to be forever drawing 'lines in the sand' and making 'statements'. With my notoriously long memory, I won't soon forget when Barry Hall was tying up his shoelace and the North players decided to push him over. They followed up with some ultra-courageous jostling and bumping as the Big Bad Bustling One attempted to leave the arena while three or four of them held him down in a headlock. This, apparently, is what's known as the Shinboner Spirit.

It is hardly unexpected, then, when before the first bounce a group of North Melbourne Fake Tough Guys attempt to rough up The Bont. Our Golden Boy had committed a heinous sin in the strange world of footy ethics: he had taken exception to the fact that in our previous encounter with North, Lindsay Thomas had laid a head-high tackle on Lachie Hunter. One which put Lachie in hospital overnight.

In the interests of fairness, let's explore The Bont's outrageous accusations in full: 'We didn't really like it at all, we thought there was quite a bit of malice in it. [Hunter] will be okay, hopefully he can relax and be okay over the next couple of days. But we thought it was quite a bit unfair.' Shame, Bont, shame!

A few things soon emerge as significant flaws in North's master plan. (I am positive, and indeed Brad Scott later admits, that it was an orchestrated attack.) The problem is, though The Bont may not be Barry Hall (he has a lot more hair for one thing), nor is he a raw-boned and spindly 18-year-old anymore. While, like a fond parent, I still haven't quite adjusted to the fact, The Bont stands shoulder-to-shoulder with many ruckmen. He's an imposing 93 kilograms now, so he is far from daunted by the physicality of the North players. Nobody – least of all Michael 'Spud' Firrito – puts Bonti in the corner.

I always feel that The Bont is a mysterious mix of calm and competitive. While the burning, intense desire to win is virtually imprinted on the faces of some players (the Liberatores, both senior and junior, come to mind), The Bont always appears serene and unruffled. He looks as though footy is still, somehow, just a game – albeit one he is stupendously good at. His power, rather like our former champ Chris Grant, is in his grace, rather than brute force. And yet, as Firrito and his gang are about to find out, and as Joel Selwood discovered last week, it is unwise to overlook the competitive spirit of Marcus Bontempelli.

But there are more things to worry about than how The Bont will stand up to the attempted intimidation. Last time we played, the Kangaroos had beaten us by 16 points; it felt like more. And the names we are missing from that day are too painful even to contemplate. Yet, during the week, Bevo Our Saviour had said, when asked if this Dogs group could still win the flag, 'You try telling them they can't.'

I try to hold that thought in my mind even as we make a poor start, even as, again, the question of how we can scrounge enough goals looms, and we go close to a goalless quarter. Then, after this shaky beginning, the perennially unlucky Clay Smith goes down with concussion, and we find ourselves in a far too familiar situation: a man down for the match.

Through sheer grit we gain the lead early in the second quarter (and won't lose it again). Goals are still hard to come by. With Jake the Lair somehow still mysteriously subdued, new sources must, and do, bob up. There's one bloke, for example, who juggles a one-handed mark at centre half-forward before going back and slotting a long goal – it's none other than the composed and lionhearted fan favourite, Celeb Daniel.

With North seething like a swarm of frustrated, angry ants, there's a push-and-shove show of strength involving all players at half time.

The Bulldogs crowd pulses with indignation. There is in reality so little that we supporters can do to affect the game's outcome (leaving aside talk of lucky scarves and Bonti badges). We yearn sometimes to show the players how much we're with them, to give them our thanks, to share their disappointments and sorrows, to demonstrate – in this case – our anger. But we can't leap the fence and put one of the North antagonists in a headlock; the petite stature of the Libba Sisters would render this impossible in any case.

But we can show them we're with them, and part of them, so we launch into a chant: *Bulldogs! Bulldogs! Bulldogs!* It thunders around the stadium. It's primal and raw. People who in real life are mild-mannered and gentle are yelling it out at the top of their voices. Grandmothers, teenagers, nurses, teachers, people with uni degrees, pensioners, students. Kids whose cots were once draped with Bulldogs scarves. People who've lived all their lives in the western suburbs, as well as people who've only recently taken up the faith. Refugees and new arrivals to our country, for whom it's all a dazzling and intriguing spectacle and a bewildering blur. People who've never seen a Bulldogs flag. People who have. But it's oh so long ago. *Bulldogs! Bulldogs! Bulldogs!* The warring tribes separate, with little harm done, and retreat to their own caves.

Do our efforts have any impact? Do they elevate and inspire Our Boys, as we hope? Or are we, the fans, just white noise rumbling in the background, barely relevant to the tight little cocoon of players and coaches and injured teammates? We all resume our seats, perhaps a little sheepishly, before going in search of our half-time snacks.

Our Boys go further ahead in the third quarter. Twenty points up at the last break doesn't really reflect the dominance we've established. It's a lot, however, in the context of this low-scoring affair, where for the maimed and injured Dogs each goal reflects dozens of gutsy and selfless acts. But the lead is far from insurmountable. We squirm in our seats and almost wish for another scuffle to break out.

With audacious faith in his troops, Bevo places 20-year-old Lukas Webb and 19-year-old Josh Dunkley in the centre square to begin the last quarter, on which are riding our finals aspirations, our very 2016 season. It's strange, and a little poignant – and a whole lot scary – to see these kids in the thick of the action, instead of the comparatively grizzled old hands Wally and Libba. But Josh and Lukas are undaunted. They're not there to play bit parts, despite their fresh faces and their light frames.

Nevertheless, our run has slowed. Fatigue has set in. It's a scrappy, tough arm-wrestle. North gets two frees in front of goal. Brad Scott's reaction is not shown on the TV screens. Our defence is besieged, but the 2016 Men's Department is so much more than the sum of its individual players. The reliable duo of Boyd and Morris know where to be, and how to direct the youngsters around them. The raw, ungainly Fletcher Roberts keeps learning and growing, game by game, quarter by quarter, from these stalwarts. And we have the magnificent Easton Wood; these tight last quarters seem made for his bold reading of the play, his spectacular intercept marking.

But still I feel the familiar, jittery panic. It is not shared by Our Boys, these young men whose single-minded belief is fiercer than I've seen in any Dogs team, ever before. *You try telling them they can't.*

The siren goes, and our brave and injury-stricken team have defied the odds magnificently again. The players head over to the cheer squad, stopping for the frequent selfies that are requested, for the brief touch of hands, those little moments that connect the fans with their dream. Our dream.

We hope, but don't really know, that in some way we spurred them on. That our chant, ringing around the arena, played just a tiny part in their motivation. That it showed them we know how tough their footy lives are at the moment, that we've grieved with them as player after player became injured. Rattled the opposition with the strength of our unity, fans and players alike.

The boys sing the song a bit more raucously than usual. We've won a torrid physical battle, triumphing over the physical tactics and trash talk with which North tried, and failed, to intimidate us. The win cements our place in the finals. That it makes our rivals' position in the eight that bit more precarious – well, there's a grim satisfaction in that too.

The Bont gives a TV interview. The 56-game veteran deflects attention modestly back to 'the kids who've stepped up'. The Bont had 19 disposals. Not many by his peerless standards, yet to my mind he was, if not the best, then at least the most influential player on the ground.

There was a priceless moment early in the match, right in front of where my tribe sit. Spud Firrito had the ball, close to the boundary, and tried to launch a booming kick out of the danger zone of our forward line. But The Bont was right there, and with an athletic leap and full deployment of those 'go-go-gadget' arms, he spoiled the kick and forced the ball out of bounds. Spud looked crestfallen, while The Bont's reaction, which was visible only to we who were facing the two players, was a sight to behold. There was jubilation, and a full and utter appreciation of everything the moment meant. And there was a touch of that facial expression which generations of mothers have threatened to wipe off their children's faces: a smirk.

Among all the sublime and audacious things The Bont did tonight – the nine tackles, the long, raking kicks, the strong contested marks – that smirk might very well have been the thing that delighted me the most.

THE POINT OF IT ALL

When the Dogs take on the Pies I am on holidays, catching some sun, a couple of thousand kilometres away. I'm hoping against hope for one of those uneventful, comfortable, slightly dull wins. Scraping home in all those close matches has been thrilling, but I'm ready for just one match in which our worst complaint is that we took our foot off the pedal in the last quarter. I want to have the luxury of grumbling that we should have been building percentage. It would be an unaccustomed relief if, during the last quarter, with the game well in our keeping, an earnest debate could begin: who should be in or out of the team for the next week based purely on form, instead of through necessity as another injury strikes. I'd like occasionally to feign condescending admiration for the opposition's efforts. 'Some good kids there. That Darcy Moore looks a likely type, doesn't he?' Maybe even – but only if we've won by at least 15 goals – I could graciously say: 'I'm looking forward to seeing that kid's career unfold.'

Such indulgences are rarely the Bulldogs' lot. Certainly not in the second half of 2016. And so, inevitably, early in the third quarter against Collingwood we are struggling badly, down for the count. The weight of injuries, that perplexingly dire forward setup, the absence of Dale Morris to corral the defensive troops – all these things and more are painfully apparent. Around the ground we appear flat, careworn, bereft of answers.

Too often we've seen Dogs teams meekly surrender these must-win games. But we didn't have Marcus Bontempelli then. We've had champions, plenty of them; for us, through long years of failure and disappointment, savouring the gifts of individuals was often our only consolation. But I'm not sure we've had some-one like The Bont. Someone whose own indomitable will and competitiveness, allied with sublime skills, can single-handedly swing a game. It may be a strange analogy, but he sometimes reminds me of those mothers who somehow find the strength to lift a Volkswagen to free their trapped children.

Emboldened by The Bont's feats (of both varieties) in his flashy lime-green boots, everyone around him becomes inspired. Liam Picken, who shows a particular relish when playing the Pies, his father's old team, locks down the dangerous Steele Sidebottom. The aftershocks of his crunching tackles shudder through the stadium, even reaching me as I pace around the room in Far North Queensland.

And yet, though we bridge the three-goal gap, we can't shake the Pies off. I'm far away from my Bulldog family, and from my actual family as well, as the last quarter crawls by. It's a peculiar torture watching it on TV, the awful camera angles ensuring you have no idea whether it's going to be a Bulldog player who first lopes into the frame or several Magpies ready to link up smartly down the centre of the ground. You have no idea whether a desperate shanked kick was the best one of our players could do because of suffocating pressure, or whether he'd overlooked Bulldogs teammates leading purposefully into space. (This seems unlikely, given the current sad plight of our forward line, but if I were at the game at least I'd know.)

We dominate, but without impact. We lock down and fight and scrap time and again; our spirit, our effort, can't be faulted. We're ahead, still, and there are 30 seconds to go. We should be safe. (But wait – wasn't that the sliver of time in which we managed to snatch the game from Sydney's clutches just a few short weeks ago?)

There's a random free kick to the Pies, followed by another random free kick to the Pies. It's all too speedy even for the obligatory outrage, because the ball is being launched into the Collingwood forward line. Just the scenario in which the promising young Darcy Moore might take one of his wretchedly promising marks, 30 metres out. But it's Bulldogs hands that reach the ball first – safe hands, those of Roughead and Matthew Boyd. They pump it forward, and That Flashy Man Who Likes to Show Off, who'd looked a bit more his old self when he went onto the ball in the last quarter, takes a mark right on the siren. We used to not know how to win; now it's as though we don't know how to lose.

Afterwards, I learn that this win has made history. It's the first time since 1946 we've beaten the Pies four times in a row. That's quite something, when you consider a dire statistic: in 153 matches against the Pies we have won only 46 times.

I work out that our current 'streak' began in June 2014. And I'm almost instantly transported back to that game. It's one that stands out from the rest, even though it should have been just a meaningless, mid-season, humdrum home-and-away match. Nothing of note was riding on it. Hope of an improved year for the rebuilding Dogs had long since faded. We were well down the ladder, coming off a bad loss from which it was hard to eke out even one positive, while the buoyant Pies were in great form and finals-bound.

On the morning of our encounter, I'd been by turns distressed, angry and resigned when a stinging article had appeared in *The Age*. Our club was labelled 'irrelevant'. The Dogs, with their unattractive, grinding, blue-collar game plan, generated no excitement, the article opined; we had no stars and were further away from a flag than ever.

There was further demoralisation in that week of low points. Bob Murphy in his regular column took a gentle but pointed gibe at those fans who were becoming increasingly restive as the losses piled up. He reflected on better times: 'Some of my most treasured time in football has been at the top. Winning big games, winning finals, playing in front of huge crowds when you can actually feel the pride of your own supporters beaming back at you, like the warmth of the springtime sun.'

His words seemed at that moment those of someone who had fallen out of love with the game – or, more chillingly, with our club. It felt like he'd reached a fatalistic acceptance that those good times, when the team was playing well and when we as fans basked in that winning afterglow, were beyond reach of this current group. Or at least a group that would still feature a Bob Murphy, with his sidestep, his elegance, his sublime talent. His crazy-brave passion for our club. Which, right then, was giving him more pain than joy.

Against this gloomy backdrop, the family text messages to
organise our attendance at that 2014 match against the Pies
weren't exactly zinging around.

'You going?'

'Umm. We probably should.'

'Yeah. It's important, right?'

'Even though we'll probably get smashed.'

'There's that, yes.'

'Meet you at the usual fate.' (Oops, damn autocorrect!) 'Usual
gate!'

The reason I got myself off the couch and trudged up La
Trobe Street towards that 'usual fate' has sustained me through
decades of Bulldogs non-achievement. You don't get to pick and
choose when to barrack for your club, disappearing from their
orbit in the bad years, only to reappear with suspiciously new
scarves in better times. Going along every week in these hard
times forms a protective fortress. It's our own way of bearing
witness. And it will make our triumph one day (it will happen
one day ... won't it?) all the more poignant and unbelievably
sweet. And – it's what you do, that's all.

There were few Dogs fans around. So few that we all kept
catching each other's eyes. It felt like we should exchange some
terse acknowledgement. Laconic and Australian.

'You're here too?'

'Yep.'

Nothing else required.

While waiting for family members at the 'usual fate', I got
talking to an elderly, rheumy-eyed man wearing a Bulldogs
beanie. He looked too old to be there on his own; he was hampered by a limp. We made small talk: the weather, a few mildly

jocular observations concerning Pies fans and ticket prices. I
wanted to ask him why he was there, about the things he'd seen.
Had he been there in '54? Who was the greatest Bulldog he'd
seen? What did he think of our current plight? I was sure he
had a story to tell. But I hesitated, and he headed into the stadium with a cheery wave.

I'd recognised another Bulldog-supporting couple walking
in. They usually sat a few rows in front of us at home games.
We'd never spoken, but I'd watched their joy when we won, seen
them jubilantly waving their scarves and singing the song, and
shared their quiet resignation when we lost. I felt strangely glad
to see them. To know that they were here too, compelled like
me by reasons both complex and simple.

Only four members of my clan went to the match that
day. One brother. One sister. One son. And me. We were
deliriously happy to see that we were in front at quarter time!
In time-honoured 'acceptance of mediocrity' mode, we'd
jumped enthusiastically to our feet to give Our Boys a clap.
At three-quarter time we were still somehow six points up.
We glanced at each other, with a nervous tentative happiness,
far from jubilation. It was only when we got the first two goals
of the last quarter that it really occurred to me we might actually win.

Just as I was grasping this unlikely possibility, the Pies began
an ominous charge. Their uncharacteristically subdued fans
began their famous scary roar, as their players clicked smoothly
into a higher gear. Maybe the Pies had been toying with us,
waiting for this moment when the real match would begin and
they could flick the irrelevant Bulldogs away like annoying
mosquitoes.

I considered how many times the Pies had played at the MCG in blockbuster matches, with a pressure-cooker atmosphere and a huge crowd, and with so much more at stake. They were at home in this screaming cauldron, where the air seemed to have vanished, and we could barely breathe. The Dogs were about to crack. The Pies, who had everything to play for, a finals berth on the line, were steaming home, within a goal with five minutes to go. I braced for our 'usual fate'.

But there was a last lunge of Bulldog defiance, a last fierce flurry of intense contests. Somehow our team won them. Somehow we held Collingwood off, and launched our own counter-attack. When the siren went, our joy knew no bounds. Amid the din, you could have easily forgotten there were probably only 3000 of us Dogs fans there. I remembered something else Murph had said in his article, about strength in hard times: 'You suddenly find yourselves a tightly wound-together group of human beings who genuinely feel like it's you against the world.'

The four of us took a photo of ourselves celebrating wildly, to capture forever the memory of The Day that We Were There.

There was a new kid playing just his sixth game for us that day. His composure and decision-making would later earn him a Rising Star nomination. He was still a bit clumsy, but there was something indefinable that caught your eye. Would his nickname be The Bont or Bonti? The players were so convinced of his talent, we'd heard, that they called him 'Footch'. For our future.

The importance of being there, the mystery of why fans of unsuccessful clubs endure – these thoughts, on which I often muse, have been on my mind for another reason. Last week, after our win against the Kangaroos, some not-so-funny banter was directed at us by a North Melbourne supporter. This person – let's call him Shinboner – jeered at us that North had won four flags in his lifetime and then launched that not-so-thorny, not-so-tough question: 'How many flags in yours?'

Yes, Shinboner had us there. I have to confess that I did not need to consult Wikipedia, do a Google search or resort to finger counting to come to the answer. But as an evasive politician might say to a journalist's grilling, I don't accept the premise of the question. While the heartache of our failures is raw and can't be denied, something more than a simple win–loss ratio is what connects a football team and its supporters. It's the 'something' that compelled us to be there on that June day in 2014.

A Bulldogs premiership – especially after an epic wait of at least 61 years (thanks for reminding me, Shinboner) – will be precious indeed. But I imagine that a flag, mysteriously enough, won't drastically change anything essential about my feelings for our club, or even be the thing that sustains me when the wheel of footy fortune dumps us back down the ladder again one day.

We can make a choice to go to a well-reviewed movie or walk out of a disappointing restaurant. And yet we will stoically attend matches in which our team is certain to lose, where we know the outcome is likely to be depression, frustration and even anger – just because. We front up, week after week, during those tedious seasons where the writing is on the wall virtually from Round 1. We can – and do – question our sanity, wonder exactly why we're wasting our 'leisure' time on something that is so frequently … well, unenjoyable.

Whenever I watch the Dogs, layers of memory are always, always there. They form a collage of sounds and sights and even, for those of us old enough to have seen matches at the Western Oval, smells. The losses, the wins. The years of just being there.

Like all Dogs fans, I feel a sense of awe and slight disbelief that, even though it's unlikely to be this year, the day may yet come when we are part of the excited, nervous throng filing into the MCG on grand final day. We imagine Our Boys lining up for the anthem, the MCG a sea of red, white and blue. I wish I could explain to Shinboner that those miserable days – the days of heartbreak, our failures – won't be forgotten or swept aside in our joy and tears when that happens; in fact, somehow they will be the point of it all.

CARPE DIEM

You could say we have a love-hate relationship with Essendon, our neighbours from the posh side of the Maribyrnong, but if I'm honest it's mainly been hate. In one year alone, they defeated us by over 100 points. Twice. Regrettably, I was present on both occasions. The Bombers' fans revelled in our humiliation, one of them ceaselessly calling for the Windy Hill gates to be locked to keep us in and prolong our suffering.

So, in Round 21, 2000, when the Dogs spoiled the Dons' opportunity to go through the season undefeated, we celebrated with over-the-top glee. The fact that we proclaimed this, a mere home-and-away win, as the most memorable victory we'd ever witnessed undoubtedly deepened the scorn that the Bombers, with 16 premierships locked away in their trophy cabinet, felt for their pathetic neighbours from the wrong side of the tracks.

Now, as we meet in 2016, the Dons have been enfeebled by a drugs scandal. The plight of our mortal enemies has brought no sympathy from Bulldogs fans – though we share the broader football world's anger that it ever happened, and disgust at its impact on their players. There's still a sense that the club, known for its hubris, is in denial about what's gone on. Before our match their chief executive explains, straight-faced, that the club will ask the AFL to reward it with a Round 1 feature match in 2017, saying, 'Everyone would acknowledge we have been a special case this year.'

And then the Bombers come out onto the ground against us, running through their banner, which, with no sense of irony, promotes the James Hird Academy, which – apparently – nurtures young talent.

The repercussions of the drugs saga linger for more than just Essendon alone. In the equivalent match in 2015 we'd defeated the Bombers, prior to their drugs suspensions, by 87 points. Former Essendon player turned Bulldog Stewart Crameri was best on ground, kicking seven goals, which some uncharitable Bulldogs fans were quick to point out was more than the entire Essendon team that day. (Crameri was booed all night by the Essendon fans. As one Bulldog wit explained, 'They don't like drug cheats.')

The absence today of Crameri, who like his former teammates is serving a 12-month suspension, is a factor in our struggle to rack up a respectable score. The cumulative effect of our injuries is also painfully apparent. With so many missing, goals are hard to come by. I feel strangely sad watching the wreckage of the Men of Mayhem style, as we labour, with more determination than skill, to a 40-point victory.

I have to remind myself that despite the media's romanticism of the brave young Bombers' efforts, the team that was desperately youthful and inexperienced was not the one donning the sash. More than half our team – 13 players – have played fewer than 50 games, compared to 10 in the red and black.

One of the Bombers' players out there is playing his 250th and final game. It's our former star and Brownlow medallist Adam Cooney. At the end of the game Adam waves his thanks to the Bulldogs fans, before whom he'd played more than 200 of those matches. The poignancy of that moment – along with our flat and uninspired performance, and the fact that yet another key player has been struck down by injury (this time Easton Wood) – sends my thoughts drifting into some familiar, if unwelcome, territory: the dangerous assumption that there will be limitless chances for a talented group like ours to grab a flag.

We should know this better than most: there is no orderly queue for success. The fact that we will finish towards the front of the line in 2016 does not guarantee a smooth pathway to a flag the next season, or the one after that. Too many hurdles and random factors, things we can control and things we can't, await to trip us up.

Adam Cooney was a number-one draft pick in 2003, a laconic character with a shock of wild red hair. He had elite skills and explosive pace. We were dazzled by the potential of 'Coons' and his two close mates, Farren Ray (number four in the same draft) and Ryan Griffen. They were the new, unafraid group who, we believed, would lead us to premiership glory under second-year coach Rodney Eade. (He was called Our Mastermind, not Our Saviour. But the sentiments and hopes were the same.)

With the shiver of apprehension and superstition which is the ever-present legacy of an Irish-Catholic upbringing, I wonder: did we have the same investment, the same belief in their boundless potential, their capacity to keep improving, which we now have in the precocious talents of the 2016 group?

Lately I've become resigned to the idea that we are simply too injury-ravaged to make a tilt at the flag this year. But it's consoling to believe that a few tweaks to our game plan and a full and healthy list (surely our nightmare run in 2016 can never be replicated) will see the premiership drought broken in 2017, or at least 2018. But that same cold shiver, and the memory of how Cooney's career played out, tells me there are other, much less palatable pathways that the Class of 2016 may take. Because those three great hopes of the 2006 group are now finishing their football journeys at other clubs, and not one of them has tasted premiership success.

Cooney's 250-game career brought him a Brownlow, four years of finals appearances, and All-Australian honours. It also left him with a bung knee, which is what brought him to retirement at only 30 years of age. From 2008 onwards, when he was just 22, he was unable even to train. Farren Ray is now at his third AFL club, North Melbourne, where he has only been able to eke out one game. After moving from the Dogs to St Kilda, Farren at least played in three grand finals, though each of them was a loss. Ryan Griffen went on to captain our club but left with bitterness and rancour. His premiership dream remains alive – with the Acronyms.

In fact, only one of Cooney's teammates from that winning 2006 elimination final team lined up against him in Sunday's match. It was the bloke who had worn number 42. It wasn't Liam Picken, however. This player was not a number-one draft pick thoroughbred, but a rookie; maybe he was still sporting those blond tips from his days as a Frankston reserves player. Keith Boyd, at that stage a plodder compared to the more glamorous trio, was definitely not the one any of us would have predicted would last the journey. We'd never have guessed that this bloke, known for his work ethic and perseverance more than silky skills, would still be playing 10 years later, having already captained our club and won three Charles Sutton Medals. He's spending his twilight years playing career-best footy in a defensive role. You know he hasn't given up on that premiership dream.

Looking back at the careers of Adam, Farren and Ryan, who all fell out of love with our club one way or another, makes me realise that Our Boys never really remain Our Boys – and not just in the sense that Adam Cooney's magnificently unkempt mane has disappeared, and a bald spot is now prominent. History says some of the Class of 2016 won't make it. Some will find themselves on the wrong side of the end-of-season whiteboard, jigsaw pieces to be offloaded in the horse-trading, or simply delisted. Some will never be able to overcome the frailty of their minds and bodies, the attrition of our brutal game, the ever-present consequences for individual and team of a wrong decision or poor game, the relentless scrutiny of the media and the desperation of the fans.

The Bulldogs players form a guard of honour for Cooney; many knew him well but others not at all. The fans' applause for our former champion is warm and respectful. But he's no longer one of Our Boys, and Our Club is Our Club, always. Our loyalties and affections, but most of all our hopes, have moved on. Now we have a new number 17. Maybe the Dogs' biggest, boldest gamble for premiership success, the enigmatic Tom Boyd, who just this week turned 21.

This week I watched a video on the club's website showing the bond between players who've worn the same number. The latest features The Bont with Daniel Cross. Yep, I was the one who made the maudlin claim, when Crossy was forcibly retired, that I could never, *ever* love another player as much as the ultimate team man, the bravest of the brave, Daniel Cross. It turns out, of course, that wasn't quite true.

Despite being cut from the club after 210 games and playing two more seasons with Melbourne, Crossy is one of those rare players whose passion for our club rivals that of the fans. I have an ache in my heart when he confides that he used to kiss his guernsey before each match. The Bont listens to him respectfully, taking in the words of his predecessor in number four, the man whose name he sees every day on his Whitten Oval locker. 'It's great to be able to catch up with past players who have worn the jumper,' the younger man says, 'to understand their level of love, care and compassion for the jumper, because it makes wearing it even more worthwhile.'

For us fans, there is always another year in our epic wait. Whatever happens in 2016, we still have a next year in which to live through the whole range of footballing emotions: expectant, pessimistic, realistic, grouchy, frustrated, uplifted, despondent, ecstatic, buoyant, proud, despairing. Often in the one match. Frequently in the one quarter. Our journey will go on as another season always beckons. The players' time as Bulldogs, though, is short. We smile and shake our heads every year as we see the earnest, fresh-faced recruits awkwardly parading in their brand-new jumpers, with their skinny little arms and wide-eyed innocence at having made it to the big time. They think they have all the time in the world.

Marcus Bontempelli, barely out of his teens, will captain our club again this week now that Wood has gone down. I feel that little shiver again, thinking about it, and imagining the silent message conveyed by all those names on the lockers that he and his teammates see every day. Of not taking anything for granted. Of grabbing our 2016 opportunities – even if they appear to have been blighted by injury – and seizing the day. We can never be sure when and if it will come again.

FAR FROM THE MADDING CROWD

It's the final round of 2016. Though the sides that would constitute the final eight have been well established for a couple of weeks, in the last round there's a topsy-turvy game of snakes and ladders going on to decide the final ladder positions. The Dogs can either finish in the top four, with a double chance, or face a sudden-death final, potentially interstate.

Given the signs of fatigue and our horrible injury list, we need to hope that the results will fall our way. In other words, it's time to fear a creaky intervention from that invisible driver of the Bulldogs' misfortunes: Ole Tom is surely ready to step from the shadows.

He's already wielded far too much influence through his diabolical intervention in Round 3, that awful moment when Bob did his knee. Imagine if the last 60 seconds of the game had been different and we'd defeated the Hawks. Even if every other kick, handball, umpiring decision and catastrophic injury for our club then played out in exactly the same way in every 2016 game that followed, we would have been perched in third spot. Our destiny, though Ole Tom would never actually allow this to happen, would have been securely in our own hands.

Instead we spend Round 23 riding the coattails of other clubs which can influence where we land. We are reliant upon a series of unlikely results to ensure a home final for us, despite the fact that our total of 15 wins would, in many seasons, have comfortably ensured a top four position.

Improbably, for all of us who endured The Preliminary Final that Must Not Be Named and The Other Preliminary Final that Wasn't Very Good Either, we must firstly barrack for the Adelaide Crows. Yes, our fortunes depend on the sound of that theme song, the stuff of nightmares and post-traumatic stress disorder symptoms, ringing out triumphantly at the end of the match. If That Certain Team from South Australia defeats the Eagles, our chances of a home final improve significantly. However, not for the first time, the Crows fail to fulfil their role in the script of a Bulldogs fairytale.

Shamelessly, we transfer our hopes onto North Melbourne; we need them to defeat the Acronyms. Sure, it's unpalatable at first, but before long I begin uttering the words 'Go, Boomer, you little champ' and 'That's another great spoil from Firrito'. I begin emulating some theatrical gesticulations from Brad Scott, and exclaim at regular intervals: 'I can't believe the umpires missed that head-high tackle on Lindsay Thomas!'

When these efforts fail, I come to a realisation: 'It's not them. It's me.'

I am too crushed to throw my support behind the Magpies. In the unlikely event that they defeat the Hawks, we will swap places, assuming the Dogs defeat the Dockers in Perth in the very last match of the round. Our match will be played an hour behind the Pies–Hawks clash in Melbourne. Given that the Hawks are certain to prevail, I've already begun to fret about just what carnage Josh Kennedy, Specialist Bulldog Wrecker, might do to our team.

Yet with minutes to go at the MCG, the Pies are on the verge of an amazing upset. They have snatched the lead from the Three-Peaters. For seconds, just seconds, we glimpse a parallel universe in which the Dogs have a smidgen of luck. But then a Melbourne reject in his first appearance for the Hawks breaks out of the centre and launches a long kick.

Perhaps the oval ball will stand awkwardly on its point and take an unexpected 90-degree turn. There could be a random swirl of wind, a 1997-style goal umpire gaffe. Something, anything, could intervene, and yet as it sails perfectly towards the goals I know there will be only one outcome, the perfect Thomas Hardy twist. Of course the wretched luck of the dying seconds of Round 3 will have a mirror image in Round 23. Of course it will inevitably be the Hawks snatching this win and ripping a home final from our outstretched hands.

I turn my attention back to our own match, which is now underway in Perth. It isn't pretty. We launch ragged forays into a forward line that is either empty or features Celeb Daniel as our sole marking target. It is impossible to believe we are the same daredevil team that blitzed Freo in Round 1, so long ago.

That's because, in actual fact, we are most certainly NOT the same team. Since that faraway day, eight other first-choice players besides Murph have been consigned to sit on the sidelines. And on Sunday, every single weakness in our armoury – our youth and inexperience, the lack of cohesion that comes from too much turnover of personnel – is on display as we crash to an embarrassing defeat.

The result of the match doesn't actually matter. Once I realise that it's a dead rubber I most certainly don't want to see any brave efforts. In fact I'm calling for the whole team to don tracksuits and do a Nick Kyrgios and concede the match. Given that's unlikely to happen, there would have been comfort in cruising to a comfortable victory at this ground, where our record is frankly abominable.

Because now we know we'll be returning to Perth, to the AFL's most formidable interstate venue, in 10 days' time, to play the Eagles. They are in blistering form and now viewed as likely grand finalists, in an elimination final. And our club has never won an interstate final. We will be playing in the most hostile of environments, far from the energy and enthusiasm of our fans, without our chants, cheers, jeers and (if necessary) boos, which we fondly believe give our players that extra edge, the impetus to keep running in a tight last quarter, to make one more leap, one more tackle.

Yet despite everything, footy fans – and especially Dogs fans – are built to endure. And even though no team has ever won the flag from seventh on the ladder, and the idea that our brave but bruised kids could rewrite that statistic is preposterous, slowly our despondency begins to lift. In defiance of whatever hideous plot twist Ole Tom has in store, our thoughts swing back to optimism. I begin counting the reasons that we could pull off the upset of the century.

Our captain, Easton 'Superman' Wood, is likely to return. He'll be ready to fly, time and again, in the path of the bearded full-forward who just loves kicking goals against the Bulldogs.

If we ditch our 'away' strip, those infernal white jumpers – which I'm convinced, without any solid evidence, are unlucky – we're a five-goal-better side. Jake the Lair has been serving his penance in the VFL. With a point to prove, he could play a blinder. There are a few whispers that Libba the Second, whose season was said to be over, may somehow return. If he's there, his ferocious presence around those packs, his brutal attack on man and ball, it's bound to lift us even further. What better way to smash our Bulldogs fatalism to smithereens than by somehow claiming a heroic win in Perth?

I think of our performance against Geelong a few weeks ago: unexpected, gallant and brave. I recall the many matches this season when, although not at our best, we've somehow found a way to win. The expressions on those young faces as they huddle together pre-match, or lock their eyes on Bevo's as he rallies them at three-quarter time.

I remember what I said in Round 3, when we thought Bob's injury had ended not just his season but his career. It was more of a prayer than a statement. It's relevant right now too, as we prepare to face the near-impossible task of beating the Eagles.

Surely it can't end this way. Not even Ole Tom could be so cruel.

'TRY TELLING THEM THEY CAN'T'

'It always seems impossible until it's done.'

Nelson Mandela

'Why not us?'

Marcus Bontempelli

'THIS STORY IS OUR STORY'

As usual, it was Bob who said it best. Our sudden-death final against the Eagles, he judged, would be all about belief. 'We don't have to manufacture it,' Bob said. 'It's already there.'

My own belief, I know, is a more fragile thing. Too many times it has been trampled in the dust, exposed ruthlessly in finals on the big stage, in the big moment. Too many times there's been heartbreak. Too many times the Dogs teams in which we've placed our dreams have not been up to the task.

I've been there for all seven preliminary final losses, all the way back to 1985. Some were devastating, some were humiliating. Again and again I've rekindled my faith in a different future, every time a new wave of bright young talent came through. I've seen those hopes dissolve like a cruel mirage before our eyes.

And yet at some magical moment in the 2015 fairytale season I made a conscious decision to jump on that rollercoaster again. I'd strapped myself in, eyes scrunched shut, doubt and fear banished – if not fully, then at least as far away as a battle-scarred Bulldogs fan could manage. I signed over, again, my peace of mind to a bunch of blokes running around a football field. For who could resist this new breed's enthusiasm, their joy in playing beside each other, their talent, their determination to write a new narrative for our club?

And so, despite the way we'd limped to the finish line in 2016, I listened to the fighting words coming out of the Kennel in the lead-up to Thursday night's final with hope, and beat down my own cynicism. I resolutely shut away the doubts that threatened to creep in whenever I heard (over and over) those dismal statistics about our record of winning interstate games, in particular our horrid recent record in Perth. Not to mention the endless recital of how many goals a certain bearded full-forward wearing number 17 had kicked against us.

I blocked out, as best I could, the memory of the one and only match I'd ever attended in Perth. It was 1991. I'd arrived late due to a delayed flight. A chuckling taxi driver was delighted to inform me that the Eagles had already kicked seven goals without the Dogs troubling the scoreboard. Peter Sumich, one of a series of swarthy, pirate-style Eagle forwards who particularly relished playing the Dogs, went on to kick 13. His tally alone was double what our entire team could muster. West Coast slaughtered us by 113 points. The crashing wave of the Eagles chant and the claustrophobic roar of a one-team venue are my lasting memories of the night. Unsurprisingly, I've never returned.

But all that's in the past, I tell myself, as I prepare to ride the wave of belief that Bevo Our Saviour and our team keep talking about.

'I'm itching to get out there,' says Dale Morris.

Dale has played 226 games. Missed 18 months with a broken leg. Played 10 finals, of which we've won only three. Achieved just one Brownlow vote. Kicked three goals, in his whole career. Dale's smile is as wide as any starry-eyed first-gamer as he says those words.

Five players are returning to the team which looked lost, and out of ideas, against Freo. Bevo wouldn't commit the cardinal sin of finals and risk unfit players ... would he? But ... does Libba look like he's limping as he collects his bags from the carousel at the Perth airport? Is Jackson Macrae's face, as he steps down from the team bus, that of a young man who is fit, determined and focused, or of one who's unsure if that hamstring which tore so badly will hold tight when he starts loping around in his characteristic way? Sheez! This striving for positivity stuff is exhausting.

The Libba Sisters take up our now traditional positions on the couch in the Rising Sun apartment. We have a proud record of 100 per cent success here. At least that's one stat in the Dogs' favour this week. The Eagles have won 16 of their last 17 matches in Perth. They've kicked over 100 points in their last four games. The last time we kicked over 100 points was a lifetime ago, in July. We had only managed a pitiful 49 in our last game in Perth.

Across the road from my sister's apartment, the Whitten Oval field of dreams stands silent, dark, eerily empty. More than 2000 kilometres from our western-suburbs heartland, our players line up for the anthem. I'm trying to decipher their faces, read their expressions. Is that nervous tension or steely self-belief?

And why on earth has a line, mangled from the Paul Kelly song 'To Her Door', popped into my brain? Can Our Boys 'make a picture, and get it all to fit'?

In the first few minutes, three easy chances for our Dogs to score are fluffed. In a sudden-death final, maybe we won't get too many more of these relatively simple opportunities. And then we botch what should be a simple clearance out of the defence, and Shane Biggs launches a kick that nestles gently onto the chest of That Bearded Full-Forward we've all been trying extremely hard not to think about all week. Then the Eagles quickly surge forward for another goal. For all our hard work, we're exactly where we feared we'd be: goalless and trailing.

What follows is something that I feel may just transform our club forever.

Instead of dropping their heads, their morale slowly seeping away, the Dogs ramp up their energy. So many opportunities are created that a goal surely has to come. Liam Picken, the gentle father who dances to *Frozen* with his three kids during the week, but who morphs into a blank-faced competitive beast on the field, has started brilliantly; he's the man to spark us after a gutsy contested mark. When his goal sails through, something is unleashed in our team.

The Men of Mayhem make a dizzying, triumphant return.

As well as Liam, relentless pesky mosquitoes such as Celeb Daniel, Luke Dahlhaus and Clay Smith swarm everywhere. Our tackles are immense, extraordinary. The skills that had all but vanished throughout the grey gloom of winter are back. Slow, hesitant ball movement, tentative forays forward, fumbles and overuse of handballs – well, apparently that was *so* Round 23.

When I'd decided pre-match that I must follow Our Boys' mantra and simply 'believe', I was anticipating a low-scoring, dour arm-wrestle. Something like a 42–39 result. We would be gritty, determined; we'd strangle the Eagles with our pressure. Instead, the Dogs blast nine unanswered goals.

There isn't much conversation between the Libba Sisters at half time. The Eagles, we are sure, will regroup, come at us hard. Matthew Boyd had said pre-match that it would be critical to silence the crowd. 'Over there,' Keith had said, 'silence is golden.' But when the Eagles hit their stride, that cacophony of sound will begin. Our stunning form has been too good to be true, while the Eagles' performance has been stunningly bad. The only question is whether, and how, we can withstand the challenge that is bound to come.

Sure enough, in the second half, the Dogs are put under pressure. But it's only fleeting. The Eagles' rally is unconvincing. Our fanatical efforts snuff it out before it really comes to life.

There's a critical turning point when the Eagles centre the ball to a player alone in the middle of the ground. Out of nowhere comes Shane Biggs, taking the enormous risk of leaving his opponent, to effect a spoil. A player materialises to rove that spoil as cleanly as though it's a training drill. It's Celeb Daniel, who has been everywhere, his skills razor-sharp, his vision always acute. We goal from the fast break, quelling the immediate danger.

A minute or two later Jordan Roughead takes a powerful mark 60 metres out. Before we can speculate on what he might do, our brave-hearted ruckman pivots around with the nimbleness of a rover and roosts a wonderful goal. His teammates run from every part of the ground to celebrate.

It's only in retrospect I realise that, even though it's only halfway through the third quarter, this was the moment the game was well and truly won. We were there, you see, for The Preliminary

Final that Must Not Be Named. I know the Libbas aren't the only anxious ones even now, when we are six goals ahead; our fans everywhere – in bars, lounge rooms, in all corners of Australia – are nervously checking the time, pacing and prowling, mentally calculating ridiculous and far-fetched possibilities, Ole Tom–style scenarios. A power failure could force the match to be replayed. A wrongly completed team sheet might mean an overly zealous AFL official could dramatically rule us ineligible. Our score might revert to zero because of a botched interchange.

But the Dogs themselves are untroubled by these bizarre thoughts and hunt the ball as avidly as ever. Our lead builds, out past 40 points. I don't even know I am still holding my breath, until The Bont kicks a monster goal 20 minutes into the last quarter and points to his chest. For heart. For belief.

I notice for the first time that a sound has slowly been building. The Dogs fans who somehow got to the match are small in number, but their chants are reverberating around the stadium as the Eagles supporters begin to depart.

It feels like we have been waiting for this win forever.

The Libbas count down the seconds, our arms around each other, till the siren sounds. A commentator says: 'Who would have believed in their wildest dreams that the Dogs could win so convincingly?'

We know the answer. Our Boys did.

They make their way off the field after acknowledging the small group of deliriously happy fans. They pound out our song. We sing it as well. Our voices wobble with tears.

There are so many stories in the Bulldogs' rooms.

Of best on ground Celeb Daniel, who was constantly overlooked and derided for his height.

Of Joel Hamling, who was unable to break into the team for most of the year but is now singing the song with extra vim. His opponent, That Bearded Full-Forward, managed only 13 ... points in total.

Of Libba the Second, who missed last year, and came back, and then busted his ribs, and then had wire put around the two broken bones in his ankle so he could be out there. Our former captain Luke Darcy reckoned only one per cent of players could have played through the pain he did.

Of Bob, who walked around the boundary touching hands with our fans. His composure faltered only once: when he embraced Matthew Boyd in the rooms.

Of Luke Beveridge, the journeyman player. His mysterious alchemy with our players and our club has brought us this moment.

There are stories within stories, too, of the people celebrating in the rooms with Our Boys.

There's John Schultz, the gentle ruckman and elder Bulldogs statesman. He played in our last grand final, 55 years ago this month. He couldn't have foreseen, as we lost that game, that our club would have failed to feature in another for so long. Or that he himself would never experience the excitement of a final again. He is a revered figure around our club, sending beautiful heartfelt emails to the players. Celeb says: 'He's the best man I've ever met. I love him to bits.'

There's Rohan Smith, our formerly dashing half-back who now oversees a stingy team defence. Rohan's 300th – and last – game was in 2006, a final against the Eagles, at this very ground, when yet another of those swarthy Eagles pirates, Quinten Lynch, bagged six goals. We lost by 74 points.

There's Daniel Southern. Daniel played in three losing finals in a short, injury-riddled career in the 1990s. He is often infamously remembered for the headlock he applied on Peter Sumich during a wild brawl in 1994. Rohan Smith, Lachie Hunter's dad, Mark, and Libba the First – all were Daniel's teammates that day. As was a player wearing number 19 and a mullet, Luke Beveridge. And the brawl was sparked by a fair but bone-jarring shirtfront applied by Mitch Wallis's dad, Steve.

But to us Daniel Southern is not a person of infamy, but a quirky, thoughtful man who converted to Islam and narrowly escaped the chaos of the 2011 Egyptian Revolution. The man who had to retire at the age of only 25, with knees that were completely shot. Daniel Southern is the defender, sidelined by injury, pictured crying in the MCG grandstand after his teammates lost The Preliminary Final that Must Not Be Named. I guess we'll never know if his presence – maybe just one timely fist punching away one of those Crows forward entries – would have been enough to thwart that two-point loss which has haunted us for so long.

We see Daniel embracing Tony Liberatore, his 1997 teammate and the littlest, feistiest Bulldog of all. His legacy continues in the competitive, iron will that he's passed onto his gifted son Tom.

Seeing these men together with the winning team is like a collage of our past, present and future. A Footscray/Western Bulldogs dreaming, with the poignancy of a Leunig cartoon.

Later, the club releases some behind-the-scenes footage. We get to see the boys in the room with Bevo, post-match. You can see the coach's emotion as he thanks the playing group; they seem so heartbreakingly young off the field. They really did 'make that picture, and get it all to fit'. We, the fans, we're just bystanders watching. There's a look in their eyes that makes my heart catch in my throat.

Luke tells them they've been brave, that they made each other, and us, proud. 'This story is our story,' he says. 'And it's got a long way to go.'

THE DAYDREAM BELIEVERS

In the Western Bulldogs museum at the Whitten Oval, there is a wonderful photo of a group of excited young Footscray fans, camping out the night before the 1961 grand final. I can't help thinking they were lucky, though, that their vehicle, festooned with flags and banners, was not a DeLorean, able to catapult them forward to the 2016 future and a glimpse of the Dogs' fortunes in the 55 years that lay between.

At the optimistic moment in which their exuberant celebrations were captured, the team from the west were about to compete in their second grand final in seven years. Footscray's captain-coach was the charismatic excitement machine of the era, E.J. Whitten. These buoyant young men, with their sign reading 'Bulldogs for Premiers 1961', would have expected the good times to keep rolling on. They would have been astonished and dismayed to learn about the barren years their team was about to endure. That there would be no more flags, in 1961 or thereafter. Not even one grand final appearance.

In stark contrast, during that same period the Hawthorn team, which overcame a half-time deficit to defeat us for their first ever flag, went on to win 12 more.

The festive group, hunkered down in their sleeping bags – though I doubt any sleeping followed – would have been dismayed to learn it would be 24 long years before the Dogs even returned to the MCG to feature in a final. (We lost two in the 1970s in the miserable grey concrete surrounds of Arctic Park.) The Hawks – by then with five premiership cups in their trophy cabinet – awaited us once again.

The year was 1985. It was the first time, since I started going to matches as a four-year-old, that I'd even seen our team in a final. When the Footscray boys ran out onto the famous ground to a tremendous roar, I saw people openly weeping. Whether with joy that this day had finally come or sadness that it had taken so long, it was impossible to say. There were tears of a different kind when the Hawks demolished us by a humiliating 93 points.

I push these thoughts behind me as I go to collect Stephanie for our 2016 showdown with the Hawks. She opens the front door, wearing her jumper, her badges, her bright hopes. 'Let's do this!' my 12-year-old niece says.

Stephanie and the Libba Sisters join the Dogs fans marching from Federation Square to the G, a place for us of great pain and few triumphs. The mood as thousands of us walk along is both excited and tense. We've floated on air since last week's magnificent win. But we worry – we're extremely good at worrying – if that victory was our grand final, a match our battered team had psyched themselves up for. We fear – because we're also very used to being afraid – that we may not find that same determination and belief yet again, taking on this powerhouse opponent.

Inside the famous ground, the formidable might and power of the Hawks, who've dominated the competition since the 1970s, are on full display. Brown and gold flags circle the arena. Footage on the big screen shows their many recent triumphs, on a loop.

We're in a part of the ground dominated by Hawthorn fans. They look – of course – unflustered, calm … smug is really the word I'm reaching for. I look at them with fear and envy, thinking how different their experiences have been to ours, how few disappointments they've ever endured, how quickly their minor setbacks have been transformed into triumph. How used they are to winning.

Our two teams have always had little in common. One from the leafy east, the other from the gritty west. A commentator once described that chasm: 'The shoppers from Forges meet the shoppers from Georges.'

Tonight the Hawks' banner features a glitzy high-tech holograph photo. Their club has posted a profit of more than $3 million for each of the past three years. Their membership tops 70,000. They exude money, entitlement and success. My long memory for injustice and slights against my team is reactivated. In 1989, one of the Hawks' countless premiership years, I recall standing in the outer of Princes Park, the Hawks' home ground, as they predictably annihilated us. We were surrounded by pimply faced private schoolboys. (You could just tell – take it from me.) Our club was on the brink of extinction: the attempted merger/takeover was only weeks away, though we didn't know it then. As a Footscray player made yet another miskick, one of those callow private schoolboys jeered at us: 'Out on the full. Just like their club.' My western-suburbs hackles begin to rise at the memory.

It's a monster crowd. The Three-Peaters are accustomed to this atmosphere, the big-game aura. But only two other Footscray/Western Bulldogs teams have played in front of crowds bigger than this: the '54 premiers, of course, and the '61 grand finalists.

The 2016 Bulldogs start well, but in an unsettling sign Tory Dickson, our most reliable kick, misses two sitters. The Hawks sweep the ball away, scoring two goals with imperious ease. As we try to settle into the tempo of the match, there's one of those 'it could only happen to us' moments. Toby McLean snaps a goal. But even as we celebrate we see Luke Hodge remonstrating with the umpire, adamant that it's been touched. There's a scoreboard review and the goal is overturned.

The incident has all the elements to fit perfectly into the long litany of Bulldogs hard-luck tales and western-suburbs grievances. A Danny from Droop Street moment. ('Of course they'd listen to what Hodgey the good bloke says, but never to us!' I can almost hear Danny say.) It could have turned the match. ('Just like that bloody Riewoldt free in the 2009 preliminary final,' Danny groans.) It could have arrested our momentum, sparked caution and doubts. It could have been lamented and discussed forever, like the growing mythology around the Tony Liberatore point/goal in the last quarter of The Preliminary Final that Must Not Be Named. ('I was sitting right near the point post. It sailed straight through the big sticks,' Danny maintains.)

This white noise, this ceaseless chatter that always rattles around in the minds of us fans, is so fatiguing. Our Boys are listening to a different beat. It's the one Bevo Our Saviour keeps talking about. They refuse to hear anything that tells them that a premiership is not their destiny.

Because of this burning belief, Our Boys view the Hodge decision as an irritation, a hiccup early in a match which still has a long way to run. (In fact, later, we benefit from a similar overrule, though this would have been unlikely to mollify Danny.) Cyril Rioli's tackles as he twice creeps up on our players and runs them down from behind are something to learn from, mistakes not to be repeated. They won't inhibit us, stifle our run and carry, spark doubts that might spread through our troops like an insidious disease.

With goals from The Bont and The Lair, we launch another spirited challenge at the Hawks early in the second quarter. The Bont's goal comes from a glorious moment when he outbodies Luke Hodge, the elite player who symbolises the Hawks' success and glory. Still, whenever we draw close, the Hawks are able to swat us away. They extend their lead to 23 points; they are unruffled professionals absorbing our pressure, then coolly returning fire when their chances inevitably come.

I feel a seed of doubt germinating. We've flung everything in our arsenal at them, but against this opposition perhaps it will never be enough. Sixteen of their team, after all, have played more than 100 games; we have just seven. Shaun Burgoyne alone has played in 33 finals – more than the total games of fresh-faced Josh Dunkley, Celeb Daniel, 'In-Zaine' Cordy, Joel Hamling and Toby Mclean. The Hawks' line-up is studded with men whose legends will go on forever, men who have played in four premierships, men with Norm Smith Medals.

Just before these excuses crystallise in my mind and my old defensive pessimism sets in, we make another surge forward. Clay Smith marks the ball. He lines up for a crucial shot, perhaps 40 metres out, to keep us in the match. We know Clay has an awkward, some would say ugly, kicking action – just as we know he has an enormous heart. But when we've imagined these clutch moments, these absolutely critical opportunities, we've hoped it would be The Bont or Jake, our blue-chip talent, with the ball in hand.

But this moment requires more than talent. It also requires a fanatical self-belief, an inner strength forged in the worst kind of adversity. These are traits on which Clay had to draw as he endured all those knee reconstructions. Maybe, as he went from surgery to crutches to those first tentative laps around the Whitten Oval, the dream of a moment just like this helped him along. He's the right man to take the shot after all. His kick sails right through.

Clay's goal ignites his teammates yet again. Nineteen-year-old Josh Dunkley has been just about our best player in the first half, unfazed by the football royalty in brown and gold, laying crunching, fearless tackles, never intimidated when it's his time to stand in the centre square against triple premiership heroes. He kicks a goal, and our unlikely star forward, Clay, bobs up irrepressibly for another. We're pressing hard.

There's a stoush at half time, with us now just one point down. The Hawks attempt to send a statement to the impudent upstarts, to restore the rightful order and quell this latest, and most unlikely, source of insurrection.

Often in these situations I've quailed at the sight of our team being pushed around by bruisers with a streak of mean. But Our Boys are far from being intimidated, acquiring extra zest and energy, jostling right back and getting in the faces of the exponents of 'unsociable football'. Liam Picken positively bristles with excitement at the chance to be in the thick of it, while whatever Libba the Second is saying to the Hawthorn aristocrats gets right under their skins. There may also have been – in fact I'm sure I saw – a vintage Bontempelli smirk.

It reminds me of the melee that broke out at half time in that famous victory in 2000 against the Bombers, in which we ended their unbeaten season. And just like on that celebrated occasion, when even the ever-smiling Brad Johnson was seen to mouth expletives, Our Boys are galvanised, rather than diminished. The scuffle brings out that same spirit, that same glee at having successfully unsettled their rivals, that same togetherness as they eventually regroup and march together off the field, mates and brothers who aren't going to take shit from anyone. Our captain, Easton Wood, is bouncing on his toes as he leads them into the rooms.

I don't know at that point if we will win. But I am confident that if we lose, timidity won't be the reason. This will not be one of those ghastly finals spectacles – one of them was against just this mob in a horror display in 2008 – where our stage-fright, our unpreparedness for the physicality of a final, are embarrassingly laid bare.

That the Dogs then embark on a third-quarter rampage is beyond our wildest hopes. The Hawks can't get their hands on the footy, or on any of our players, as fleet-footed men in red, white and blue storm in waves down the field, and manic forwards trap the ball in our zone as though their lives depend on it.

The Hawthorn edifice is swaying in the wind, about to topple like the statues that are symbolically pulled down by marauding revolutionaries.

The moment we finally hit the lead is like the release of a pressure valve. Our Boys now throw caution to the wind, playing thrilling, brilliant footy.

Not coincidentally, we see the welcome return of the Jake the Lair strut. There's a moment that only he could manage, a fraction of an instant in which, amid the frenetic whirl of action, he slams the ball to boot. It's never going to miss. We are pulled from our seats as though magnets are attached to our heads. Fans in the jewel-like colours of red, white and blue form a backdrop of arms raised in the air. The Lair doesn't even look at the goals before his celebration begins. Pandemonium breaks out. It sounds, for one glorious moment, as though every one of those 87,000 people is cheering for the Dogs.

We've dreamt of seeing The Bont take over the MCG stage. It's even better than we hoped and imagined. There are two big moments when he effortlessly outclasses Luke Hodge. It really is the old buck against the new buck. The passing of a baton.

Unlike last week against West Coast, we're there to share these moments with our magical team, who build an ever greater lead. Our eyes shine with unshed tears. We feel that ridiculous pride at their performance, as though we've brought it about, we who have never stood in front of a rampaging forward, never placed our heads over a ball, never had to keep running when our legs are burning with lactic acid. But we share it nonetheless, at an MCG where suddenly there is more red, white and blue than brown and gold.

We defeat the Hawks by 23 points, the first time we have won two finals in a row since – yes – 1961.

Stephanie and Joel rush down to the fence when the siren sounds. They're rewarded with high-fives from two of their idols, Easton Wood and 'Celeb' Daniel.

At this ground, this time last year, when we lost to Adelaide in an elimination final, Stephanie cried heartbroken tears. I think about the two kind men who consoled her, telling her that this was just one year too early, that next year would be the one. Somewhere in the crowd, those two are surely belting out our song, just as we are, for the umpteenth time.

And what of those starry-eyed young men who camped out in sleeping bags in 1961, expecting a glorious future stretching ahead? They'd be into their seventies now, I guess, but I like to think they are here in the celebrating crowd too. Older. Wiser. A touch sadder. Believers, keepers of the faith.

It's poignant, among all the joyful chaos, to see Bob Murphy out there embracing his boys. Bob had kicked the footy around in the pre-game warm-up, linked arms in the tight circle of the Men's Department huddle as tactics were plotted and intentions were pledged. But when our team was struggling in the first quarter, Bob was as powerless as the rest of us, a mere spectator, hoping that Easton Wood would nail – as he did – that clichéd 'captain's goal' to finally get us on the board.

There's so much to think about as I join the throng that marches again, this time away from the G and back to the city. It's not a raucous or triumphant crowd. People are lost in a rev-erie. The thought that we are scared to voice has crept into our minds: that maybe, just maybe, this could be our year.

I'm thinking about fate, and belief. This week, I know, we will hear story after story about those seven preliminary finals that we lost, by a little or a lot. Were they the result of dastardly planetary alignments, abominable umpiring, AFL conspiracies? Is there some wretched, yet-to-be-identified curse on our club, the equivalent of the 'Curse of the Billy Goat' that afflicts the Chicago Cubs in the Major League Baseball? (They haven't won a World Series since 1908, or played in one since 1945. My kind of team, in other words.) Or could it be the case – though it seems so boringly prosaic – that those other Bulldogs teams simply weren't quite good enough? And that perhaps, at last, this one is?

Culture, someone once said, is about 'the stories we tell ourselves'. If the players are to smash their way through the Bulldogs' culture, then the fans' stories of heartache and disappointment – the very glue that binds us to our club – must become, to them, as remote and irrelevant as the sepia photos of the Prince Imperials that they walk past every day.

I start to think about the preliminary final next week – to be played against the Acronyms. They don't have our history, in which hundreds of players have worn our colours and thousands of fans have barracked for more than 130 years. Though the Acronyms are free of our baggage, they also have none of our soul.

I listen to snippets of conversations from my fellow fans as we walk. About who was our best, besides The Bont. (Maybe Jack Macrae, or Liam Picken?) Of when we realised the match was won. (The answer, of course: the final siren.) There's murmured talk about whether to make our way to Sydney to see our team, to be there alongside them, these magnificent daydream believers. Because now our team is just one win away from a grand final. That rollercoaster is clicking on its tracks, and we're all strapped in for dear life.

It has been a rainy, gloomy week in Melbourne, but it feels like spring as we walk together alongside the Yarra, a community of Bulldogs fans and their dreams. There's a full moon peeking out from the clouds. The skyline is dazzlingly lit, and our city has never looked quite so beautiful.

WHY NOT US?

The First Quarter: Looking for a sign

Within an hour of our magnificent win against the Hawks, we Bulldogs fans have decided. We know we have to somehow be there for the preliminary final.

We look up flights and research hotels and fret about tickets, all of us who've seen those three consecutive preliminary finals failures. All of us who remained stoic, and present, during our slow and hesitant rebuild. We who had shared such shock and disbelief when a beloved captain walked out to play for this club that now stands between us and a grand final. As we make our preparations to travel to Sydney, even though nothing can ever really erase the heartache of all those lost preliminary finals, we refuse to listen to the ghosts that whisper that it could happen again.

We cling to the words of The Bont. With a cavalier disregard for our sorry history, our young champ says that he and his team carry with them the belief and motto: 'Why not us? Why can't it be us?'

And even though I could personally rattle off dozens of reasons why this sort of glory has never quite seemed 'for the likes of us', we make our choice and begin to ask that same question, but in a different and more hopeful way, a way we never have before. We move forward, almost trance-like believers, hitching our ride to this unlikely daydream. No team has won the flag from seventh. But The Bont said: 'Why not us?'

So we organise our tickets for this final, which will be played hundreds of miles away in Sydney's west. We meet up at an ungodly hour on Friday morning to make the nine-hour trek. Three car-loads of my family are driving up. The kids have face paint. We all have hope.

Everywhere on the long, boring stretch of the Hume, we see our red, white and blue colours flying proudly. There's a lump in my throat whenever we stop for a break and I see how many other large family groups are on the same epic quest as us. People drape their scarves and pose for photos in front of the 'Dog on the Tucker Box' at Gundagai. Flash cars and battlers' cars are all making this pilgrimage, kids waving out the back at people they don't know. Fellow travellers in every sense.

I'm on the road with my fellow Libba Sister, of course. We're in rollicking high spirits, on the alert for signs and omens as the miles fly by. We pass Beveridge, and Sutton, and Murphy Creek, and a town called Ruffy. Cordeaux is obviously a French twist on Cordy. The towns with unusual names don't faze us either. 'Mittagong? I'm sure I've read it's an Aboriginal word for Western Bulldogs!'

We bypass any songs that are sad and maudlin on the sound system and sing along, loudly, to those that are uplifting and inspiring. We're with Aretha in an off-key version of 'I Say a

Little Prayer'. We join Paul Kelly as he sings about being high on the hill, looking over the bridge to the MCG.

The live version of 'The Boxer' comes on. Just like the Central Park crowd, we sing 'lie la lie', the chorus, with all our hearts, the beautiful anthem of defiance, pain, struggle and resilience.

The Second Quarter: A Harbour City awash with red, white and blue

We're staying in Parramatta. On Saturday morning we ease our nerves by taking the ferry to Circular Quay. They say 10,000 of our supporters have made the trip. We see at least 9995 of them.

We strike up conversations everywhere we go with our fellow true believers. 'How did you get here? Where are you staying? Do you know how to get to the ground?' But for some reason I can't quite explain, we don't talk about the game, or match-ups, or how we might win, or whether we will win.

I don't see a single fan of the Acronyms before the match.

It was inevitable, our two teams meeting like this, fated, after the ugliness of the Griffen switch, after the ill-will of Callan Ward's poaching. It will mean something, this victory, whether it's the club with tradition, struggle and heartbreak that prevails, or the team that's had it all handed to them on a plate. As the ferry ploughs its way back to Parramatta, I watch a father with his arms wrapped protectively around his young son. Both are lost in thought, both are wearing Bulldogs jumpers, both have number four on their backs.

The Third Quarter: Of families, and stories

We find our way to the stadium. The Dogs' fans outnumber those of the Giants. We really have come via planes, trains and automobiles to be here, so many hundreds of kilometres from home.

My family takes up a whole row. I've seen each of the younger family members cry with anger, pain and mortification when the Dogs have shattered their hopes and dreams – and even in their young lives, this has been far too frequent. They used to wear number 14 for Callan Ward, and wrote him a letter asking him not to leave the Dogs to play for the Giants. Now they have Luke Dahlhaus badges and Easton Wood's numbers on their backs.

I'm not wearing the Bontempelli badge that I bought when I made the grand prediction, in just his third game, that our number four would one day captain the club, win a Brownlow and a Norm Smith Medal, quite possibly in the same year. I've brought another talisman, though. I'm wearing a treasured necklace that my father gave to my mother for her 21st birthday.

My mother is here today. There aren't too many games she's missed since she saw that '54 flag and rashly anointed the Dogs as her team. She is 79 years old, but a citizen of the digital age, of course. Deciphering the baffling text messages she sends after each game is a family sport, with their non-auto-corrected phrases such as: 'That was a dairy tale!'

My dad, the talented rover who played for the Footscray reserves, is not here. He was just 46 when he passed away. It was still the era of 12 Melbourne teams, suburban grounds and Saturday afternoon footy. I can't quite imagine what Dad would have thought, if he'd known that a Footscray team would be playing for a grand final spot in a twilight final against a five-year-old team in the outskirts of Sydney. He would have been amused, perhaps chuffed, to know that his children and grandchildren have driven nine hours to follow the team to this unlikely football outpost.

We all have stories such as these, the hordes that embarked on this journey, who are now sitting on the edges of our seats, restless, anxious, hopeful, patient and yearning. Always yearning.

The Giants' big screen keeps telling us: 'Our time is now.' Probably, as our banner cheekily suggests, the phrase tested well in Greater Western Sydney's 'stakeholder' focus groups, when the AFL began to plot another stage in its strategic plan, a premiership for a team in orange.

My sister, looking around at the thousands who've joined us in our long journey, says, 'Surely our hearts can't get broken yet again.'

I'm not sure if it's a question or a statement, but either way I don't have an answer.

Now we are all rising to our feet, at the first sign that our players are running out for their warm-up. We sit down, grinning sheepishly. Word has spread among the enthusiastic crowd: it was only two club officials coming down the race.

Minutes later, though, our team actually does run out, to a huge wall of sound. A 'Bulldogs!' chant reverberates around the arena. Again, and again, and again. We are loud, so loud, louder than even last week at the G, we fans who have so often been timid, introverted, always ready to retreat into our shells and await a new misfortune.

The first goal is kicked by Clay Smith, the man who now wears the jumper which Callan Ward relinquished to go north. We don't know yet the story of Clay's week: that he is mourning a close mate who died tragically just days previously. Clay plays a heroic first quarter – he's a human wrecking ball, throwing himself into kamikaze situations, tackling as though – well, he knows better than most – each game could be his last.

There are two Giants fans sitting – I'm not sure why – among our Bulldogs contingent. One of them calls out, monotonously, whenever he perceives that the Dogs have lost a contest: 'They don't want it.' Which just goes to show that the Giants' supporters, who think their 'time is now', have an awful lot to learn about this game of ours.

The Fourth Quarter: A game is being played

The Giants are 14 points up, a few minutes into the last quarter. It's the biggest lead of a seesawing night. Ghosts from preliminary finals past are rattling, hard, at our window. We have missed too many shots. We've made countless forward entries. Not enough of them have resulted in goals.

There have been herculean efforts all over the ground. We gasped in awe when Easton Wood soared majestically in a brilliant, high-flying first quarter. We'd seen our defence stand tall against the Number-One Draft Picks. With Easton in the trenches, Matthew Boyd and Dale Morris have marshalled and supported their young and inexperienced teammates in the 'Men's Department'. While the Acronyms' Heath Shaw launches tantrums and abuse if a mistake is made, our senior men give just a tap on the arm, a word of encouragement. Fletcher Roberts couldn't have imagined he would play a final this year after spending most of the season at Footscray. Now, though he has had his nose smashed early on, he has worked tirelessly to keep the Giants' glamour forward Jeremy Cameron to only a couple of possessions.

Clay Smith has continued his manic attack on the ball, and notched up four goals. Luke Dahlhaus and Liam Picken have committed so many desperate, barely noticed acts, smothering, fighting, scrapping for every ball. Tom Boyd has gamely shouldered all the rucking responsibilities and covered enormous territory, hauling his large frame around the ground on this warm and taxing night. His makeshift rucking partner has been In-Zaine Cordy. They're both doing their bit against the man-mountain Shane Mumford, who refused to shake the hand of Jordan Roughead before the start of the game in a display of the fake-tough-guy machismo that I find particularly childish. Roughie, who's grown in stature through each week of the finals, was sidelined in the second quarter when hit full-force in the face by the ball. We have struggled in the ruck but still kept winning and clearing the ball, mainly because, despite the insights of the Giants fan near us, we simply just wanted it more.

Yet now we've fallen behind. I can't bear to look along our row, to see the stricken faces of Stephanie and Joel. To contemplate an eighth preliminary final loss.

There are only 20 more minutes to play, and the Acronyms have the momentum. They should be fresher. They've had the week off, and should have more run. The outcome takes on an inevitable shape, the script running to predetermined plan. Brave, plucky Bulldogs. Not quite there. Not ready yet. A bit unlucky, but after all, hasn't our history always been, as a certain Carlton president once said, one of 'tragedy'? Maybe there will be next year for the good old unthreatening battlers from Melbourne's west. Or maybe not.

Every Bulldogs fan finds their thoughts flickering for an instant – or more – to the pain of a loss.

Every Bulldogs player is thinking something else entirely: *Why not us?*

Our Boys go forward. Again. And again. Tired legs that must feel like concrete somehow find another step. Our players – who on average are younger, despite the hype, than the Acronyms – have no thought of conceding, no plans to settle for heroic failure.

All night the Bulldogs chant has rocked the stadium. In these minutes when the match threatens to slide from our keeping, it's frenetic, that noise. The emotion of our fans, our crazy-brave statement in coming here – we are sure it will somehow help push Our Boys across the line.

We claw back a goal through Tory Dickson. Then somehow Matthew Boyd hacks the ball out of the air to get it to JJ. He's on the wing but we're already out of our seats, urging him on as he gallops ahead with his electrifying pace. He launches the ball to the one player who's left in our forward line. That player is none other than the hero of a thousand little boys and girls, and even of a person who somehow left her badge at home: Marcus Bontempelli.

The moments in which The Bont makes his characteristic long strides towards the bouncing, spinning ball, hotly pursued by a man clad in orange, is like a microcosm of the battle between fear and belief that's always the Bulldogs' lot.

Fear: He might trip over. He might fumble. He's not, though he is so many other amazing things, especially quick. He's been hampered by an injury, and had to leave the ground for treatment. The bounce could be awkward. So many things can go wrong.

Belief: It's The Bont.

And because it's The Bont, he grabs the ball cleanly and spears the goal to put us back in front. If there's ever been a stronger, louder wave of red, white and blue emotion, I wasn't there to see it.

We scramble another goal through In-Zaine Cordy. There's still time ... but for what?

The Acronyms promptly reply. Scores are level. There's a delicate tap from The Bont, to Libba the Second. His dad, who knew preliminary final heartbreak so well, is now experiencing the same agony as each Bulldogs fan, riding every kick from the grandstand. Libba's well-placed kick lands with Jackson Macrae. He's not a noted goalkicker. Not the most likely of heroes, this unobtrusive young man. His face is pale, determined and set. Jackson Macrae kicks the nerveless clutch goal that so often our club has been unable to nail in matches like this.

There are harrowing moments, desperate acts of courage, brilliant work from our defence, to hold the Acronyms out in the longest three minutes we've ever endured. We're getting texts from friends and family in Melbourne, telling us how long it is to go. So we know, when Jake the Lair makes the best decision of his young career, not to blaze wildly at goal from the boundary but instead to centre it ever so gently so that it lands on the chest of an unattended Tory Dickson in front of goal, that there are only 30 seconds left. Tory can milk the clock. We must have it won. But it's too unbelievable to take in, even as we turn to each other, exhaling the loudest roar of relief, of ecstasy, of joy. And our tears instantly begin.

They are tears for the sorrows we have known. For the times we've left games, heads held high, valiant and brave losers, but losers nonetheless. For Chris Grant and Brad Johnson, the champions who were brave, loyal, committed, who never knew this elation. For Bob, who's out on the field crying too, our captain and heartbeat, and for the cruel fate that denied him this moment. For Matthew Boyd and Dale Morris, our heart-and-soul 30-somethings, who are now running towards the fans, their unabashed delight bringing on new waves of tears in the stands.

Families are hugging, strangers are hugging. Photos are taken. The crowd spill onto the ground, the foreign turf where Our Boys have bulldozed their way through one of the longest sporting droughts. Stephanie brings a handful of the grass where we won this famous victory back to her mother, who just can't stop crying.

Post-match: We're in the grand final

The Libba Sisters are on the road again. We keep repeating it over and over: 'We're in the grand final! We're in the grand final!'

We've watched other fans, fans of clubs newer to the competition than ours, experiencing this joy. Fans who experience it year after year, taking for granted the idea that success is always but one season away. We've been wistful, envious, shirty and downright miserable, watching them strolling the streets and looking smug in their scarves, heading off jauntily to the grand final parade.

Now we'll be doing all those things, because our Cinderella team has at last made it to the ball. And we know Our Boys aren't going to be happy just to be there.

How do these things work, I wonder, as we join thousands of other travellers, scarves waving merrily out windows, on our triumphant journey back to Melbourne? Was it our belief, our acts of faith, our wall of noise, our commitment to be there with them, that lifted Our Boys over the line? Or was it the other way around – was it their unwavering self-belief, that fierce light in their eyes, their genuine determination to write a different story from those sad old Bulldog tales, that galvanised us, that compelled us to get in our cars and travel just to be there, bearing witness as they created history with that amazing, courageous victory that will never, ever be forgotten?

There hasn't been much sleep for the Libba Sisters, but our journey is full of joy and anticipation. We turn the music up loud. There's a song we know we must play. We're in full, if rickety, voice as we sing 'Daydream Believer', flying down the Hume as though we're on wings.

THE FORCE WAS WITH US. AND WE WERE THE FORCE

It's grand final week and our Western Bulldogs' story has captured Melbourne. Our dream has swept and carried all neutral fans in a tidal wave of emotion and goodwill. There's barely a mention of our opponents, the worthy but dull Sydney Swans. We're a fable, an allegory, the good guys who everyone wants to win.

Our tale and our quest are the very definition of 'quixotic'. I know because I looked it up in the dictionary: 'Caught up in the romance of noble deeds and the pursuit of unreachable goals; idealistic without regard to practicality.'

And yet, in this happiest of weeks, all I can do is cry.

I shed tears whenever I see the words 'Bulldogs' and 'grand final' in the same sentence. And without those usual qualifying words '1961' or '1954'. Or 'never'.

I shed tears whenever I view again the incredibly moving footage that emerges of our fans' faces during the last, desperately tense minutes of that preliminary final. I recognise myself in every frame. Unable to watch, but having to watch. Unable to hope, but needing to hope.

I shed tears when in the build-up to the grand final I see the Bulldogs' logo painted onto the MCG turf. Finally we'll be at the party from which we have been excluded for so long.

Our beloved but luckless club with the most patient of fans will have the fun of going to that great Melbourne tradition, the Grand Final Parade. That happy celebration, that window of opportunity when for both clubs everything is still magically possible.

I make my way to meet my Libba Sister and set off for the big occasion, but tears fall again as I drive down Barkly Street and see the African and Vietnamese restaurants flying our colours, displaying their 'WOOF WOOF' signs.

Footscray has become unrecognisable to me these days: it's vibrantly multicultural, unexpectedly hip. In fact, the street in which my father grew up was even spruiked by real-estate agents recently as having a 'Paris end', which may perplex those who've ever visited the Champs-Élysées.

Houses in the suburb everyone used to scorn and deride now sell for a million bucks. And a new generation of young professionals, who've brought soy lattes and avocado smash to trendy cafe menus, now call West Footscray – where my parents married and I myself was christened (all in the right Catholic order of course, in case you're wondering) – WeFo.

The Libbas catch the train to the Grand Final Parade from WeFo Station. Even Metro has entered into the spirit, blaring out our song from the loudspeakers as we do battle with the Myki machine. The platform sparkles with our red, white and blue colours: there are faded, hand-knitted scarves and retro bomber jackets from the '80s, perhaps recently dragged out from cupboards but nevertheless worn with pride. There's a resurgence of the fierce Footscray and western-suburbs parochialism that I'd thought might have disappeared in our more urbane and cosmopolitan city.

I see craggy faces who look like they've been through a lot, and faces from many places across the seas who've made the western suburbs their home. Babies nestle in their mothers' arms. Children aren't the only ones wearing face-paint, tri-coloured wigs, red, white and blue nail art and hats with badges.

WeFo Station is opposite the Olympic Tyre & Rubber factory – or what's left of it, now that it's been converted to sleek new apartments. Here, both my parents and grandparents once worked. When I began attending Footscray home games, I used to wave to my Irish grandfather in his grey dust-coat. He was the gateman there. He'd been banned by his doctors from attending games because of his dicky heart, which, it was feared, would not withstand the stress of a Footscray performance. A little smile breaks through my tears.

We all alight at Parliament Station. There's a happy confusion about where to go, the best place to see the parade. We've never been here, any of us, before.

We find a vantage point that gives the petite Libba Sisters a reasonable chance of glimpsing Our Boys. I get talking to the man next to me, a newcomer from the Philippines, here on a visitor's visa. He's looking around, bemused and puzzled by us, decked out in our weird tribal gear. I struggle to explain it to him: our joyous excitement, the meaning of what is – so they say – just a game.

It probably won't make any sense to the young Filipino, but part of the answer is visible on the opposite side of the parade, where a man in our colours is holding aloft a sign: 'Here to represent parents, aunts, uncles and cousins who've passed away since 1961.' That faraway year when last a Bulldogs team made the grand final.

The parade is boisterous and fun. Members of the army band wear Bulldogs scarves over their fatigues. We're polite in our applause for the Brownlow medallist, Patrick Dangerfield, for the Swans' players and even for the umpires (because you never know). We cheer loudest, of course, for our convoy. Bevo Our Saviour, Bob Murphy and Easton Wood are crammed into the first car, where only two seats should be as Bob's name is not on the car. It's a statement that Bob is part of this journey, every bit of the way.

I study Our Boys' faces. Keith Boyd looks tense; we expect no less of our driven, competitive, hard-nosed former captain. There's starry-eyed innocence on the face of 19-year-old Josh Dunkley, whose 17 games so far have included three consecutive finals victories, and who's about to play in a grand final, something that eluded five players – Grant, Johnson, Smith, Hawkins and West – who each played more than 300 games for us.

The Bont, at 20 much more of a seasoned professional than Josh, tells reporters he's 'keeping it simple' and 'enjoying the moment'. Such is his relaxed composure that we believe him, because it was The Bont who asked 'Why not us?' and then played more than his part to make this day real.

*

The Libba Sisters make the same trip from WeFo Station the next day, our treasured grand final tickets in hand. Those pesky tears are back as I see a family group posing for a photo on the platform with their grandmother, who is frail but beaming, sitting in a wheelchair decorated with our colours.

As we walk towards the G, I realise I've barely given a thought to the actual game: the thorny question of who will match up on a certain Lance Franklin, the dilemma of how we will counter the Swans' tough, experienced midfield, how we will stack up against opponents to whom this day, with its pressures and its emotion, is much more familiar.

I can't begin to understand it but there's been a change in the strength of my faith and belief in our team. I've been more nervous, more anxious and apprehensive before many a humdrum home-and-away match. Now, I'm floating along. Happiness and delight have replaced fear. I may even, like the relaxed and affable Bont, be enjoying the moment.

I feel like I did as a child, when the training wheels came off my first bike and I took off down the street, giddy with excitement, even executing an adventurous wave in the direction of my brothers and sister.

Somehow, with me barely noticing, the weight and ghosts of failure and disappointment have ebbed away, and with them the wall of defensive pessimism designed to keep me safe from dangerous hope and flights of premiership fancy. Perhaps that pessimism was finally thrown out of the (car) window as we all, as though hypnotised, journeyed up the Hume, placing blind trust in Our Boys. Their win that night not only smashed our preliminary final hoodoo out of the park, it also cemented a magical partnership between us and our team, a circle of belief and togetherness.

The cynics, of course, are predicting a Sydney victory. The footy world reckons far too many expressions of delirious happiness from the Bulldogs' fans have occurred. The crotchety naysayers are of the view there's been too much celebration just for being *in the grand final*, even though we still haven't 'achieved anything'. This will – so they say – dull our team's hunger, make them complacent.

I think the opposite. Team and fans are in parallel. Our delight, the sight of thousands of excited fans at training, the sea of red, white and blue throughout the west, are now sweeping our team along irresistibly, even as their deeds are transforming our mindset after decades of disappointment. I know that if we lose, it will not be the result of too much celebrating or the great footy crime of 'getting ahead of ourselves', or because our players have embraced the week and worn wide smiles instead of attempting stern 'it's just another game' blank stares.

I've tried, and often failed, to imagine Our Boys running out onto the G, lifted and carried on our wall of sound. I always thought nerves and fear would be my predominant emotions. It's not the case. It's sheer joy as we rise to our feet.

For some reason, it's the sight of Our Boys quickly arranging themselves for a team photo, making room for Bevo at the front, that is the most emotional moment of all. My sister and I look at each other, not even realising our hands are gripped tight. There aren't any words. We're here. Here at last.

The Ghosts Recede

It's early in the frenetic last quarter. We went into the final break seven points up. Thirty minutes lie ahead, 30 minutes in which the 44 men out there will run and strive and push through barriers of pain and exhaustion that it's impossible for any of us who haven't played the game to understand. (I'm glad, later on, that I didn't hear at that point Bruce McAvaney's statistic, which says that we're in the box seat: only once, in the past 32 years, has a team come from behind at three-quarter time to win a premiership.)

Amid the frantic action, time somehow freezes for a moment. Many of us notice, with a strange and prescient shiver, the numbers on the scoreboard: 54 and 61.

Our brand of footy has stood up brilliantly in a brutal, gripping contest. Our Boys have never looked overawed, never stepped back from the way we've played in the past two years, since Bevo Our Saviour took over and, well, saved us, such a short but very long time ago. Our players' faces had locked onto Bevo's, during his three-quarter-time address. They were faces of men who wanted to win, more than they feared to lose.

The usual suspects have been instrumental in getting us our lead. The veterans, the backline stalwarts Boyd and Morris, have been brave, unflinching and committed leaders. Dahlhaus and Macrae have been dynamos in the midfield. The father-sons, Libba and Hunter, are grabbing with every tackle, every touch, the opportunity their dads, spectators in today's crowd, never got to taste. The Bont has not been prolific, yet each of his intersections with the game is poetic, exquisite, opening up space and opportunities that only the truly great can see.

Some more unusual suspects have got us here too. Another father-son, 19-year-old In-Zaine Cordy, playing just his eleventh game, has laid bruising tackles as a defensive forward and slotted a goal, our first for the match. Twenty-three-year-old Joel Hamling, cut from Geelong's list without ever playing a game, and having struggled to cement a spot in our team too, has eclipsed Buddy Franklin, who stands half a head taller than him and is almost 20 kilos heavier. Tom Boyd has dragged down epic marks, competed brilliantly in the ruck, and even nailed a difficult goal when pressed against the boundary.

Not one contest has been shirked by Our Boys. Not one tackle that could be made has been missed. No opportunity for a desperate lunge, or to fling their bodies into pack after pack, has been ignored.

Now, after peppering the goals in the first five minutes, here stands our team, the Western Bulldogs. The scoreboard shows those momentous numbers, 54 and 61, sending a silent message – of what, we still don't know – as the shadows begin to fall across the MCG.

Franklin marks and then slots a goal; our lead is now only a point. There's pandemonium everywhere, an enormous din rocking the stadium, and yet inside me that preternatural calm as I await what we do next and who will bring us our next goal. Somehow, now, I know – because these are our 2016 Bulldogs – that a goal will come.

There will be heroes – of that I'm sure. It's only the names, the details, that await, but it doesn't surprise me when they are revealed. Clay Smith, the human wrecking ball, will wrest the Sherrin out of the centre. The steely-eyed Jackson Macrae will lay tackles, and pump the ball forward time and again. Liam Picken will soar for a hanger. Jake the Lair will produce one spectacular moment of greatness: a one-handed pickup, before flinging the ball onto his boot in the merest fraction of time.

The Dogs are full of run, driving forward relentlessly, our history-busting team which has played three taxing finals, twice interstate, and came from behind in a ferocious preliminary final. In a superb, unforgettable passage in our forward pocket, Shane

Biggs intervenes again and again to trap the ball or get a finger-nail to it. He re-enters the fray so frequently in 15 seconds of the most suffocating pressure that you'd imagine he'd been cloned.

There is simply no way the ball is going to come out of our forward half, no matter how hard the Swans try to crash through. It becomes inevitable that the ball will spill free. Liam Picken is charging onto it. His goal puts us seven points up again.

We have even more momentum as JJ charges forward. His long kick, carried forth on a tidal wave of our roars, could be the sealer. Yet the goal is overturned on the flimsiest of evidence, without even a token protest from the Swans defenders that they had touched the ball. The vision is inconclusive at best. Ole Tom, writing our history of misfortune, may have been preparing to unleash his cruellest plot twist ever. One that would rocket right to the top of the bulging list of Bulldog hard-luck stories.

And yet, though we slump back into our seats, outraged and disbelieving, the thought that this could halt our momentum doesn't occur to me. Almost immediately, from the kick-out, Jordan Roughead takes a strong mark. There are more scram-bles, but it's still impossible for the Swans to break our will, or create a second of space that isn't filled by our red, white and blue Men of Mayhem.

It seems emblematic, when Buddy tries to burst through the centre in one last desperate foray, that the man who lunges and brings him crashing down to earth like a towering oak tree is the ultimate selfless team man, Dale Morris. Tom Boyd pounces on the loose ball and launches it towards goal from outside 50. Ole Tom Hardy has lost his vicelike grip on our story: there's no fickle, heartless bounce to wreck our dreams. The Dogs can't and won't be stopped from here.

The siren releases 62 years of pain, 62 years that we've survived with brittle humour, resignation and sometimes – it was often all we had – grim commitment. So many times we believed this day would never come. We'd learnt, painfully, to accept that such joy, such elation, would never be for the likes of us. We'd blocked out the fantasy of how this moment might look. We'd watched other teams' wild grand final celebrations at home, snapping off the TV in irritation as we wondered if we could endure another year of heartache and disappointment.

Now we're seeing Chris Grant and Rohan Smith, the faces of the 1997 heartache, weeping again, this time with joy, in just about that same spot. And now we're listening to Our Boys' names being called out, as each of them takes to the stage and becomes a premiership immortal.

Bevo speaks just the right words, of course: 'These players – their hearts are so big.' He thanks us, the fans. He says we made them feel like the Beatles at the grand final parade. 'You boost our spirits. We've ridden on your wings.' Nobody is surprised when he gives Bob Murphy his medal. We are proud, so proud, that Bevo shows that not only those who have sweated on the field this day are worthy.

Together, both these men, way back in 2014, set about healing our broken, devastated club. They both have the bigness of heart and the imagination to understand the meaning of this moment. It was right that Bevo would instinctively understand what needed to be done. And that Murph would accept it, pushed forward to the stage and kissed and hugged by his teammates who love him. He lifts the cup with the man who has led us today, Easton Wood, who with tears glittering unshed in his eyes embraces Bob.

Instead of being a forlorn and tragic figure on the sidelines, Bob runs around with the players. He lifts his match-day attire to show us that, underneath, he's wearing his jumper. It's so very Bob, and we laugh and cheer and cry because he knows what this moment means for us. Just as we know what this moment means to him.

WE RETURN TO THE FIELD OF DREAMS

'It's ridiculous what they've done.'

Former Bulldogs captain Luke Darcy

'Happy days, Richo. Happy days.'

Tom Liberatore, speaking to Channel 7's Matthew Richardson

We're queuing to get into the Whitten Oval, a long line of day-dream believers. It's a long wait. But no fans have ever been more practised in the art of patience.

The famous statue of E.J. is decked out with red, white and blue ribbons and a scarf. It's the scene of countless photos as we wait to get into our home and applaud our 2016 premiership heroes.

I listen, as the queue snakes around the ground, to snatches of conversation. Pubs in Footscray apparently ran out of beer last night; scandalously, locals were forced to consume spirits. I hear that the players had their own victory dance, which they performed after each win. It was a tradition they developed in the dark days of 2014. The music is turned up loud, the dancing is led by The Bont and Libba, and the players perform it in their undies. The lights are switched off. This ensures the modesty and encourages the participation of elder statesmen Matthew Boyd and Dale Morris.

I learn that, as well as the 54–61 scoreboard omen, there was another to give the superstitious a shiver. Our final score on grand final day, and in the preliminary final as well, was 89. The year our club was just too tough, too stubborn, to die.

I see a family group behind me and we hug like old friends. Which we are now, because they'd sat behind us at the grand final, and even their oldest family member had begun to exchange jubilant high-fives with the Libba Sisters every time Our Boys scored a goal.

We learn, with no surprise whatsoever, that Dale Morris played the entire finals season with a broken back.

Meanwhile, Danny from Droop Street has already made contact with the Coodabeens. It's all unfair, he grumbles. 'Now that we're premiers, we won't get high draft picks.'

Finally we make it inside the ground. We're standing, thousands upon thousands of us, on the turf trod by E.J. and Charlie Sutton, the men of '54 and '61. A young West Footscray rover once ran across this ground as well, a 'natural' with a 'brilliant future', who didn't make the big time. This was my father, Frank. I feel his footsteps, here, on this very ground.

Our team will be making their rock-star appearance on the balcony of what used to be the John Gent Stand, where I first fell in love with this game and this club.

All around me are stories I feel are mine, generations gathered together who've waited for this day, fans who've mainly known pity or derision, people with whom I've shared a weary glance after yet another horrid loss, people now with wet eyes and what I call the 'premiership croak'. We've all lost our voices from too much cheering and singing. We're about to do it all over again.

Our team finally come out onto the balcony, just as gloriously shabby and hungover and bleary-eyed as we'd hoped and expected. Do they know what they've done for us, the joy and gratitude we feel, that they've finally erased that terrible ache? Do they know the things we fans have been through, we who stood silently crying at this very ground 27 years ago because our team had been booted out of the competition, and then rattled tins and reached deep into our pockets? Knowing that this club meant something essential to them. Hoping, with the flimsiest of hopes, that a day like this might somehow come.

Bevo is asked whether he is a Jedi, having brought about this miracle in only his second season as coach. He says the players are Jedis – that the force was with them, no doubt.

The Bont is told that the Bulldogs' shop has sold out of his number four. He pauses for a second, as though to consider whether modesty might be the diplomatic and expected response. And then our Golden Boy gives the perfect answer: 'Well, they'd better order in some more.'

The infamous Whitten Oval gale is blowing hard, but there's sun. Of course there's sun, as we sing the song and the cup is displayed, again and again.

Looking around, I realise that tectonic plates have shifted underneath our club and its story. Because now The Preliminary

Final that Must Not Be Named, and The Other Preliminary Final that Wasn't Very Good Either don't hurt any more, having been superseded by the fresher and more wonderful memory of The Preliminary Final Where Our Boys Believed. The recurring nightmare of our preliminary finals losses and chokes and self-inflicted implosions has been replaced by the memory of Jackson Macrae nailing a clutch goal with ice-cold composure.

Stories of premierships and grand finals are no longer just nostalgic snatches of long-ago footage, with men wearing hats allowed to sit inside the boundary while the match is played. Alongside sepia pictures and the treasured reminiscences of old men, we now have 22 new heroes. Joining those fabled men of '54 and '61 are the boys of 2016, whose progress we've followed and debated and discussed from their very first games, whose tribulations and frustrations we've witnessed and shared, whose stories and heartaches and injuries and relentless self-belief have now entered our dreaming. They will be remembered, now. Forever.

And that haunting image of Rohan Smith pounding the turf in despair in 1997 has been replaced by the wondrous sight of Easton Wood creating a snow angel in the red, white and blue confetti that floated down from the 2016 premiership dais.

ACKNOWLEDGEMENTS

I would like to express my thanks and appreciation to Black Inc. Books and Julian Welch for their enthusiasm for this book and their promotion of Australian sportswriting.

I also want to thank the early readers of the *Bulldog Tragician* blog, for letting me know they enjoyed or were touched by what I had to say, and for the way they shared, followed and forwarded it far and wide to their friends, neighbours and families. It has meant so much to me whenever I heard the words: 'Your story is my story too.'

I also appreciate the fabulous *Footy Almanac* community, in which some of these stories first found a home, and especially the encouragement to new writers of its genial founder, John Harms.

For their support, help and belief in this book I would like to thank:

- My husband, Derek (the Footy Non-Believer). The Bulldogs posters and red, white and blue streamers in the front windows of our home will eventually be removed. One day.

- My three sons. The passion for, and commitment to, the Dogs of Patrick and Sean rivals my own. Daniel's doesn't, but, knowing what it meant to the rest of us, he still donned a Bulldogs scarf, took a seat in the Ponsford Stand and shed some tears with us when our day finally came.
- The Soraghan clan. From the matriarch, Dympna, to the youngest person, Joel, we have fretted, laughed, wept and celebrated the ups and a hell of a lot of downs for our Dogs over the years. I am especially lucky to have shared the Bulldogs journey – and not just that epic preliminary final road trip down the Hume Highway – every step of the way with Jackie, who's also known as the Other Libba Sister.

Snatches of conversations, witty one-liners, story vignettes and peerless nicknames thrown up by the Bulldogs crowd have been 'borrowed' over the years. Thanks to all who didn't even know they were contributing, and who might see themselves in these pages.

To Luke Beveridge and the boys and men of our second premiership, it seems impossible to describe what your deeds in 2016 meant to us, so all I can say are the simple but heartfelt words: thank you.

CPSIA information can be obtained
at www.ICGtesting.com
Printed in the USA
BVHW041215100221
599730BV00004B/965

9 781863 959254